Johnr

Intermittent Fasting

Create your new life regimen

Les Éditions JJJ

Johnny Larochelle
Intermittent Fasting
Create your new life regimen
Les Éditions JJJ

Distribution: Arrimages distribution
arrimagesdistribution@gmail.com

Graphic Illustration: Graphico-Tech
318, rue du Sud, Cowansville (Québec) Canada J2K 2X4
Layout: François Messier

ISBN 978-2-9822760-0-0
Available in digital formats:
PDF – 978-2-9822760-2-4
EPUB – 978-2-9822760-5-5

Legal deposit, 3rd quarter 2024
Bibliothèque et Archives nationales du Québec, 2024
Library and Archives Canada, 2024

Table of contents

LIST OF TABLES AND GRAPHICS

LIST OF FIGURES

Preface

Allow me to begin this story by evoking an emblematic figure, an individual whose mere mention arouses universal admiration and affection: Jean "Johnny" Larochelle.

Imagine a being whose presence is synonymous with joy, a spirit always ready for humor, and whose heart, with limitless generosity, beats to the rhythm of altruism. Johnny embodies athletic excellence, achieving perfection in disciplines as varied as golf, basketball and hockey, demonstrating extraordinary versatility and determination.

Throughout the pages of this work, you will be invited on a journey to the heart of Johnny's existence, a man who, despite the professional heights reached and the achievements that punctuated his career, remained faithful to his fundamental values.

This book reveals his intimate and incessant fight to preserve a healthy balance of life in a frenetic daily life, a struggle resonating with the aspirations and challenges of our generation.

Without pretension, but with disarming sincerity, Johnny shares the secrets of his physical transformation by highlighting the concept of intermittent fasting. This diet, devoid of a rigid framework, advocates alternation between short periods of fasting and moments of freedom from eating. This approach, although varied in its modalities, is based on scientific and physiological principles aimed at optimizing bodily and mental well-being.

This book is not just a simple biographical story: it is an invitation to reflection, a bridge between Johnny's personal story and certain contemporary societal issues, notably the global health crisis of obesity. Johnny, with rigor and humility, offers an informed analysis of this pandemic, enriched by his in-depth research and his lived experience.

Johnny's ambition linked to this publication transcends the simple sharing of experiences. True to his essence, he aspires to provide support and inspiration, revealing himself with courageous vulnerability with the sole purpose of enlightening and assisting others.

I dare to hope that the discovery of this book will give you as much emotion and enrichment as it did for me. Immerse yourself in these pages and let yourself be carried away by the force of an authentic story, that of an exceptional man: Johnny Larochelle.

Sylvain Guimond, Ph. D.

Sylvain Guimond is a doctor in sports psychology, kinesiologist, specialist in biomechanics, osteopath, and he holds a certificate in leadership and management from Harvard University.

Thanks to its posture assessment system, millions of people around the world have been helped.

He has collaborated on numerous research projects with McGill, Baylor and Stanford universities.

He is a recipient of the American Medical Review, winner of the Ernst and Young Entrepreneur Grand Prize and finalist in the OCTAS Competition for artificial intelligence.

He works with elite athletes and well-known personalities such as Mario Lemieux, Tiger Woods, Céline Dion, Gerard Butler, Arnold Schwarzenegger as well as former American President Bill Clinton. He also consults for the NHL, NBA, NFL and MLB. Sylvain is the author of several bestsellers and he delivers more than 150 conferences per year. He also served as a sports psychology consultant for the Montreal Canadiens.

Notice to the reader

Natural immunity has only one flaw: it is free!

Please consult your doctor before making major diet and lifestyle changes. If you are type 2 diabetic, a teenager aged 17 or under, or a pregnant woman, this writing is not aimed at you. I am not a qualified specialist. I am a simple citizen and retired businessman who raised two beautiful children and who has survived all the roller coasters that life throws at us at a frenzied pace, a pace that has effects on our physical fitness and our weight. The objective of this book is to tell you about my personal weight loss experience – losing 100 pounds in 7 months (now 115 pounds: reaching the goal!) – and to testify to the change in lifestyle that I am applying rigorously, a change thanks to which I maintain full control of my health and maintain my healthy weight.

With this book, I simply describe how I went about no longer experiencing the after-effects of poor nutrition and poor lifestyle habits as well as their impact on weight gain. It's up to you to see if this method suits you.

In fact, this book could be as effective as your financial advisor in fighting inflation, since your grocery bills and dining out will drop significantly. Throughout this book, I will cite the recommendations of several doctors, cardiologists and cardiovascular specialists who had nothing to sell; I affectionately call them "my good doctors". I have spent hundreds of hours researching the topic of intermittent fasting. My goal is to introduce you to a concept that has nothing sexy about it and is far from being fashionable or recommended by our governments or traditional medicine. I can also assure the reader that everything is true, because I have tested, experienced and validated it myself. I will share with you my choices and I invite you to make your own reflections, because we are all different. No pills, no injections, no specialists, no recipes prepared in advance: you must create your own new life regimen.

Yes, your new lifestyle belongs to you and you are sovereign over your body. It will allow you to finally take charge of your destiny. Understanding your body is key, and this knowledge allows you to control your life, your weight, your self-esteem and your happiness and even the happiness of those around you.

I am undertaking this journey with you for my personal pleasure, of course, but above all to share the success of this concept which consists of eating at intervals. I love writing and I admit that if I can help or inspire someone, I will be doubly happy.

This book is not a biography. Contexts, in this case mine, are important to understand the consequences of diet on our physical form. And I wish you a change in lifestyle according to your own criteria and objectives; not according to mine or those of diet salesmen and certain charlatans. Regain your self-confidence. You will boost your self-esteem by finding this simple and pure happiness.

To begin, just to break the ice, I want to prove to you that intermittent fasting does not make you sick. In fact, it's quite the opposite; this despite the reluctance of certain people. To be sure, I forced myself to carry out all the necessary medical tests after five months of this lifestyle to check its effects on myself. I can confirm that the results were eloquent as you will see below. Note that I don't take any medication... And life is beautiful!

Happy reading!

Medical Test Results

Lipides

Cholestérol	5,39 mmol/L	
Triglycérides	1,24 mmol/l	Normal
HDL cholestérol	1,47 mmol/L	Normal
Cholestérol total/HDL cholestérol	3,7 ratio	
LDL cholestérol; calculé	3,35 mmol/L	
T4 libre	16,3 pmol/L	Normal
TSH	1,49 mU/L	Normal

Fonctions hépatiques et pancréatiques

Alanine aminotransférase (ALT)	14 U/L	Normal

Glucides

Glucose à jeun	5,1 mmol/L	Normal
HbA1c/Hémoglobine totale	5 %	Normal
Commentaire	VOIR COMMENTAIRE	

Électrolytes et ions

Créatinine	80 umol/L	Normal

Marqueurs tumoraux

PSA	1,16 ug/L	Normal

Hémogramme

Méthode	AUTOMATISÉE	
Neutrophiles	2,08 10*9/L	
Lymphocytes	1,68 10*9/L	Normal
Monocytes	0,38 10*9/L	Normal
Éosinophiles	0,19 10*9/L	Normal
Basophiles	0,03 10*9/L	Normal
Érythrocytes nucléés	0 10*9/L	Normal
Volume plaquettaire moyen	9,4 fL	Normal
Indice de distribution des volumes érythrocytaires	13,9 %	Normal

Analyse et microscopie urinaire

Apparence; Urine	Limpide	
Couleur; Urine	Citrin	
Densité	1,017	Normal

Stronger And Lighter

What a shame and what a loss of potential profits for the pharmaceutical industry! I am now healthy and doctors will no longer be able to prescribe medication! Our modern doctors may be good at curing illnesses with pills, but not so good at keeping us healthy. This is not necessarily voluntary on their part: they are confined by the pharmaceutical companies in a world of medical prescriptions, this supposed fuel to good health. Not to mention that we often eat poorly and simply too much.

Finally, if you ever experience nausea, dizziness, or other uncomfortable symptoms, it doesn't mean you should or can never fast. You simply need to take a break and analyze your entire diet, then make some adjustments before completing another period of fasting.

This method is a lifestyle regimen, not a magic pill. No need to look for this pill: it simply doesn't exist!

The author and context of this book

As I have to practically lay myself bare in front of you to serve as an example, and because I had to open a multitude of personal secret drawers to prepare this book, I consider it appropriate to get the ball rolling by introducing myself and telling you some highlights of my life. This portrait will not be too biographical, but it will allow you to situate yourself in relation to my experiences, given that my journey, rich in roller coasters, may resemble that of several of my readers.

Born in Sorel, Quebec, Canada in 1963, I had the chance to experience a pampered childhood. I never lacked food, because my grandmother and my mother were excellent cooks, typically Quebecois. I was able to play several sports (basketball, hockey, golf, etc.) at elite competitive levels. I also won a few provincial championships in golf.

When I completed my master's degree in the United States in 1987, the problems of being overweight were completely absent from my mind. Once I have completed my studies, the work arrives, the real work: that of an entrepreneur. The kind of job that means long hours at work, which come with too many drive-thru meals. As a bon vivant, many happy hours to spoil myself, then return to the office, because the work day is not over.

After a few years, I feel well established as an entrepreneur. I am getting married and two children are coming to brighten up and enrich our relationship. It goes without saying that everything is still changing. Lack of time, excuses, family and financial responsibilities, everything becomes difficult to maintain, including my weight which continues to climb. At my peak in my 30s, the scale needle could swing nearly 300 pounds. Therefore I had to consult a dietitian.

I put in the required effort, I tried to cut here and there, I forced myself to move... In short, I was going around in circles and the needle was still going up; at best, it remained stable. It could go down a little, but it came back up just as quickly. This could sum up the story of my adult life.

In 2005, our family decided to take the plunge and move to Whistler, British Columbia. Without our initially suspecting it, this journey lasted four years. When I got there, I told myself that, given my obesity problem, I would never be able to climb this mountain, let alone ski down it. A reflection and a change of life were necessary, because when you are obese or too fat, you always find excuses, pretexts for not practicing certain activities. But in this village of athletes which welcomes the best skiers in the world, I could no longer hide.

I think I was the only overweight man in all of Whistler. I started riding cross-country mountain bikes, working out at the gym and, of course, skiing. To my amazement, I fell in love with this environment and, one thing led to another, my weight went from 305 to 235 pounds. I felt like a new privileged man. Everyone noticed my lifestyle change and I could now try anything that came my way, regardless of my physical condition, because I was no longer fat.

I still had a squared body; I was far from thin, but I was no longer obese. I was active all day, every day, but I couldn't maintain this crazy pace. What would happen if I changed my lifestyle or reduced the frequency and intensity of this physical activity? Yes, it would be back to square one!

In 2010, after the financial crisis of 2008-2009, it was the return to Quebec, to real work and the end of sporting activities from 9 a.m. to 5 p.m. every day. Consequence: little by little, I regained my excess weight.

I know too well the feeling of watching the scale swing up and down for years. To spare you the redundancy of ups and downs, in November 2022 I weighed 305 pounds (140 kg) again. I convinced myself to reduce my meal portions a little and go to the gym two or three times a week. I was going there reluctantly because I don't like traditional gyms. I was depriving myself of several foods and I believed that I was making efforts that would make me lose weight.

In March 2023, five months after adopting this new gym lifestyle, I am only 296 pounds (134 kg). All this time and effort for nine pounds in five months! Discouraging! I even gained three pounds by the end of March. Therefore, I stopped everything.

I no longer have the same lifestyle as in my Whistler days, either on bikes or skis all day, nor the schedule to play as many sports, because I now have to work all day. My old winning conditions are a thing of the past. I have to settle for old familiar tricks like the calorie restricted diets with cardio exercises: it doesn't work! No calorie restricted diet I know of works, none! You will understand why by reading this book.

By the way, I stopped drinking alcohol in May 2019. This gesture, positive but isolated, did not change much in my physical condition; except for my cholesterol level. But with a diet based on anything and anytime, could I hope for better?

I strongly advise everyone to stop consuming alcohol; this for the good of your liver, a crucial organ of the body. It must be said that I consider myself, despite my well-rounded 61 years, to be a sort of party animal: no need for alcohol to have fun!

More recently, I started this new lifestyle regime of intermittent fasting. On July 7, 2023, I weighed 302 pounds, while on February 7, 2024, the scale read 202 pounds. Yes, 100 pounds (45 kg) lost in 7 months! And I am 100% certain that I will never go above 200 pounds again. I have reached my healthy weight (185 pounds), a mark I will maintain until my last voyage to heaven, an end which will probably come a few years later than expected thanks to this new winning lifestyle.

Here I am now in total control of my fate. It's as if I had a switch in front of me to activate or deactivate my gestures so that the needle on my scale no longer moves.

I understand the human body better, I know myself better and I follow the best diet in the world, which fits me like a glove. I am neither a doctor nor a major specialist, but I was a victim of the propaganda system of pharmaceutical companies and the medical-economic world. I try, by choice, not to be too picky about medical data such as sugar, cholesterol or other levels. Many rely on the results obtained from their samples, but not me! I prefer to trust my feelings and my discipline, even if it means adding a general medical examination after a few months. On the other hand, I am very careful and attentive when I open the window to eat; same thing when I close it.

When it is closed, I only ingest water, without any food. Since the start of this new lifestyle, I have been perfectly aware that I must not change the times I have established for my meals during my day. At the same time, I make sure to vary so as not to accustom my body to a routine.

Just imagine: all I have to do is stick to the meal schedule set in advance in order to one day reach a healthy weight.

Where do I sign? Yes, I sign the three copies and I press hard on the pen.

Fasting represents the only natural process that allows us to detoxify ourselves, or even restore our intestinal tract, free of charge. For this purpose, to create your lifestyle with the help of reading this book, I invite you to think about a new lifestyle and you will come across this type of observations.

MY CHOICE: To no longer follow the food guide – recently unmasked, because it only serves to promote food products from multinational companies rather than good nutrition – nor old beliefs, nor the media, nor charlatans, nor pills salespeople, injections, or dietitians. Instead, listen to certain renowned cardiologists, certain cardiovascular specialists, certain university researchers, because they, unlike medical and pharmaceutical entrepreneurs, have nothing to sell us.

Your Decisive Question

Are you ready to change your life, make new lifestyle choices, stay the course, choose which foods you can keep and which ones you should eliminate and ultimately create your own personalized lifestyle plan?

We always have a choice !

The human body is hybrid

Before getting the ball rolling with the very first step of this journey, I would like to draw the best image of our human body to clearly understand how it works.

The human body is exactly like a hybrid car that runs on electricity and gasoline: it runs on glucose or fat. This simple discovery lit a light on me, because I had never thought of it.

I said to myself: what? Really? The problem is that many of us will never fuel with lipids (fat) and will run on carbohydrates (sugar) all our lives. This is how obesity sets in, causing sadly common diseases of our time such as cardiovascular problems, cancer, Alzheimer's and other dysfunctions. Everything is really connected; trust my word and that of many doctors, biologists and researchers.

So when your blood sugar (sugar) level is low and you're not eating, your body says, "OK, there's no more food coming in to give me fuel, I'm going to use my hybrid reserves (carbohydrates and lipids) and continue to function with my stored fat energy reserves instead of using sugar." It's that simple! Imagine the fat in your body as a pantry where you would go to get your fuel to supplement the carbohydrates that you would not have eaten in order to continue to function normally. This phenomenon of replacing glucose with lipids normally occurs after 14 to 16 hours of fasting. Your body will naturally change fuel types.

Historically, humans had to hunt or gather to eat. Humans couldn't call out to order a meal for delivery in 20 minutes like today. This simple concept was eye-opening for me, and I asked myself, "Why not try burning fat?" "Believe me, I lost 100 pounds in just 7 months, without ever passing out. Now, I even choose to do certain activities on an empty stomach to be more lit, more awake, to have a more alert mind. And I can also treat myself by eating a good pizza whenever I want, without overdoing it, because I have total control over the type of fuel to give to my body. There you go, as if I had just discovered a miracle at 60 years old!

It is important to understand that our brain receives 50% of its energy from glucose; the other half comes from ketones, which are produced only when the body is in ketosis, such as after about fifteen hours of fasting. Yes! Your brain will be totally on, awake, alert, in hunter mode; I could even add in cancer and Alzheimer's prevention mode. Several scientific studies confirm this. I swear I feel it when it happens in my body; so I guarantee it from my own experience. Keep this hybrid model in mind as you read this book and operate your body on both fuels; you will be amazed by the results.

Square one: the construction plan for the new lifestyle

Like any major construction or big change, it all starts with the preparation of a custom detailed plan: writing down what needs to be done and setting goals to achieve and steps to take. I would like to tell you the main points of my planning that guided me on this journey, because you too will possibly be able to see your own path in my story.

I fast forward to at least March 2022, when I had just sold part of the company I had founded. Even though I should be happy, I felt like I had just lost a child. I had a leg injury and I saw darkness everywhere. We all go through bad times; it's part of life... I was home alone, injured and weighed around 300 pounds.

The months go by, I regain a little strength; I take the bike out in the summer, but the weight doesn't move. In November 2022, I get angry and decide to join the gym, even though I don't like the good old gyms. In the following table, you will see this gym period, followed by that of the intermittent fasting lifestyle regime which begins on July 7, 2023.

Weight Loss Chart

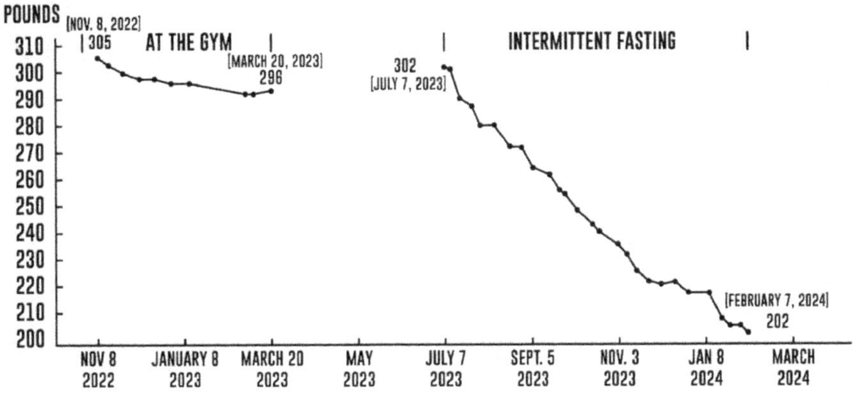

My time at the gym is traditional with a few minor food deprivations, but always a minimum of three meals a day and often with a granola bar as a snack, just to gain strength as we falsely learn all our lives.

"Eat, Johnny, you will gain strength." Rubbish! I didn't know anything about intermittent fasting, and I didn't know the common sense of giving my stomach and digestive system a break. It really is all about giving your digestive system the time to rest.

Alas, it doesn't work very well! However, I make the effort and I work out like a maniac. There was even a week when I gained three pounds: it threw me to the ground, discouraged. I gave it up. I no longer had my wonderful environment of 2005 in Whistler and I had every good excuse in the book to stagnate at 300 pounds and above, because nothing was working.

At the Gym/Intermittent Fasting

AT THE GYM	INTERMITTENT FASTING	
305 - NOVEMBER 8, 2022	302 - JULY 7, 2023	240 - NOVEMBER 3 , 2023
303 - NOVEMBER 12, 2022	300 - JULY 10, 2023	235 - NOVEMBER 10 , 2023
300 - DECEMBER 5, 2022	290 - JULY 21, 2023	231 - NOVEMBER 22 , 2023
297 - DECEMBER 12, 2022	288 - JULY 24, 2023	225 - NOVEMBER 22 , 2023
297 - DECEMBER 19, 2022	285 - JULY 28, 2023	221 - DECEMBER 1, 2023
296 - JANUARY 9, 2023	280 - AUGUST 4, 2023	220 - DECEMBER 8, 2023
296 - JANUARY 16, 2023	280 - AUGUST 11, 2023	221 - DECEMBER 15, 2023
292 - MARCH 6, 2023	272 - AUGUST 18, 2023	217 - DECEMBER 23, 2023
292 - MARCH 13, 2023	271 - AUGUST 20, 2023	217 - JANUARY 6, 2024
296 - 20 MARCH, 2023	264 - SEPTEMBER 5, 2023	207 - JANUARY 14, 2024
	262 - SEPTEMBER 8, 2023	205 - JANUARY 19, 2024
	258 - SEPTEMBER 15, 2023	205 - JANUARY 26, 2024
	256 - SEPTEMBER 22, 2023	202 - FEBRUARY 2, 2024
	255 - 4 OCTOBER, 2023	
	254 - 13 OCTOBER, 2023	
	248 - 20 OCTOBER, 2023	
	243 - 27 OCTOBER, 2023	

Comes summer 2023. I had heard about intermittent fasting and I decided to look at it more closely, out of curiosity. I had good intentions, I wanted to lose weight, but how? Running outside like crazy every day? Eating salad all the time like a rabbit? There are tons of diets on the market, magic pills and even diet ads where you can eat whatever you want without gaining weight. Isn't this unbelievable or what?

In addition, you have surely heard of miracle injections for diabetics which seem to be very successful. The problem is that we don't yet know all the side effects. And weight regain is inevitable once the injections are stopped. Nothing can beat what is natural. I began researching intermittent fasting, mainly in English, because I speak French too and some Spanish.

From one video to the next, I was pleasantly surprised. Among other things, I read the user comments at the bottom of YouTube videos, and they were at least 98% favorable. I quickly listened to several speakers and the only ones who disagreed were selling either charlatans' patents, magical gadgets, medical potions or special powders. They had no credibility.

Doctor after doctor – often including cardiologists – all praised the benefits of fasting, regardless of its duration or frequency.

The results of this cascade of positive health benefits are well documented by all kinds of studies, research and testimonials from successful people. So why didn't I know any of this? Want to know the answer? In fact, because it really doesn't pay off, nobody really makes a profit, because nothing is sold while fasting.

This opens the door wide for me. From this moment on, I make a square that I divide into four priority boxes, and I think about the activities that make me happy and that I haven't done for a long time: I therefore give them priority in my life. I no longer respected these priorities because I was too fat, I had too many excuses and I wasn't fit enough. In the end, possibly because I didn't love myself as much as I used to. You have to start by loving yourself. Here are the four steps of building my new lifestyle.

The 4 Steps Of My New Life Regimen

1) WEIGHT LOSS	2) DO A LOT OF YOGA
3) REMINISCING WITH OLD FRIENDS AND FAMILY	4) TO BE ABLE TO ACHIEVE SPORTS AND AVTIVITIES FROM MY PAST: BASKETBALL REFERRE, HOCKEY, SKI, COMPETITIVE GOLF AND SURF

These four steps are the basis of all my total makeover and become my new guide that sets milestones over time to achieve my goals one by one. I know that if I reach one, the next one will not take long and so on, domino effect. You could simply choose to walk around the block near your home, because there's no step too small, too simple or too crazy; it is your plan, for you and created by you. Take it gradually and try to choose a series of steps that increases in intensity and in which the challenge grows from one milestone to the next.

I decided not to tell anyone before trying to extend my fasting window, simply because I feared a barrage of negative comments intended to discourage me before I even started. Don't let yourself be influenced, focus your efforts on your personal new lifestyle regimen and try it for a few days to quickly feel a difference.

With that being said, let me now tell you about my four steps and the psychology behind each of them.

Step 1 – Weight loss

The first is quite obvious and we must name it; it must be at the forefront, because it is the most important. I need to lose weight at this stage before continuing my journey. If I succeed in losing excess weight, everything else will flow easily, but I must direct all my will and strength towards this goal. It's easy to write down, but in practice you will be confronted with a whole world who will throw the usual cliches at you. The first obstacles will be your close family and friends. We automatically associate the desire to please someone with making them eat or offering them something to drink, everywhere in our lives. However, no one forces us to consume; at least, I hope so. Ultimately, it is we who decide to drink and eat; the choice is always ours.

You have the right to respond negatively and make the right choices. Always!

Step 2 – Yoga

When I dropped my weight to 235 pounds in Whistler in 2005, I had reached a plateau that I was never able to break through. No matter what I did, my weight wouldn't go down. Even though I doubled my workouts or cut back on wine – I consumed alcohol during those years – my weight remained stable at 235 pounds. Today, no plateau can stop me, because I know how the body works and I can outsmart it. I succeeded because I was at 202 pounds in February 2024 (starting from 302 pounds). I just bought size 34 pants and a large t-shirt. I remain completely stunned that today I can buy clothes in this size; I could never have imagined that. In 2005, I started doing yoga after skiing and said that I found the benefits so striking that I would do it until I died. I'm not very flexible and I don't have the typical yogi profile, but I felt that it did me a lot of good. Word of a drunk who no longer drinks, I have broken my promise to myself. I knew, however, that a mixture of weight loss and intermittent fasting with yoga today would propel me towards achieving step number 4, which is to practice several sports and physical activities of my youth. So, yoga was my step number 2. For me, one helps the other and one doesn't work without the other. I would also like to point out that calm, meditation, rest and good sleep are also part of the practice of yoga. Deep long sleep is a must, even essential. It is clear that sleep brings a lot of positives to the body and mind.

Step 3 – Loved ones

Few people are well informed about the benefits of fasting and you should expect that, but you have to stay the course. I had to confront a family member following the food guide with known standard practices. You will experience confrontations with those around you, because you will be swimming against the current, but the benefits are undeniable, and I would even say that intermittent fasting is easy to accomplish once you get started. Fasting has a false reputation for making you weak, making you dizzy, and of being used only in weird religions. Nonsense! We are dealing here with a myth. However, most people are fooled and offered food for every reason imaginable; prepare yourself to ask for a simple glass of water and say, "No thanks!". Do it and you will see that it is not that difficult. Respect yourself. In the end, I concluded in my head that when someone wants to stuff me with food for no good reason, the choice is totally mine to reach a normal healthy weight instead of weighing 300 pounds. There's no doubt about it, I'm much happier with 115 pounds less weight. I am in full control of my health; no one can do it for me.

Looking back, I associate my excess weight with a lack of self-esteem which, unconsciously, may have prompted me to push away some of my friends, possibly out of shame or misplaced pride. The hand extended to those I love, past and present, should be part of my journey and prove to be a source of motivation to help me become the good old Johnny again. I didn't want to hear anything other than, "Johnny, you haven't changed." After all, I say to myself: why can't I get back to my healthy weight? Why would I be condemned to live miserably, without practicing all these sports that I loved so much? So, in my quest, I took two trips with my two best friends, while reconnecting with myself. These two friends listened to me and spoke to me; they never judged me and they avoided any confrontation. In fact, I can assure you that some people will sound negative and others will warn you not to lose too much weight. Or someone might ask you what you will do with your excess skin, another talk about how sick you look. Regardless, it won't be positive.

I told myself that Tiger Woods is 6'1" and weighs 190 pounds, just like me, and no one doubts his physique. So why doubt mine?

When you have 100 pounds to lose and you lose 20, they tell you that you're fine, not to go too fast, to be careful, not to go crazy and they throw other discouraging comments at you. But to the person next to you who is at a healthy weight, we don't tell them anything: they are considered normal.

I invite you to reach out to your friends or family, to measure the benefits of spending quality time with someone who really knows you and to reconnect in the midst of this new lifestyle process. You will get much more than just friendship, you will get a validation of your purpose in life.

Step 4 - Activities

This last step serves as a milestone on my journey, a physical progression with goals to achieve, which I consider the most rewarding for my self-esteem. I feel capable of carrying out lots of new activities and I'm not a finished man, that's a given. On July 7, 2023, at 302 pounds, I completed my first day of intermittent fasting. The first two days I felt my stomach growling and I felt something different in my digestion, but I was warned. I had done my research and knew that those first two days would have these palpable effects in my body, but I was ready. Even at 302 pounds, I was doing a lot of cycling and I clearly remember that the first two days, in a fasted state, I felt like I had plenty of energy and wanted to hit the road and do more. In reality I was recovering from a leg injury and I was lacking energy. My bike rides were certainly shorter, but on an empty stomach it looked like I had just taken steroids; nothing less! I told myself that it was indeed true, what I had learned during my research, because I felt it in my body from the first moments. After 18 hours of fasting, I have more energy, I am more awake and alert; It's pretty incredible! Incredible but true! I immediately experienced and felt it, and from that moment I never looked back. I now make it my lifestyle nothing less, I control everything and I make my choices.

However, I wanted to validate the results on the scale and, during the first three weeks, I deceived those around me: I secretly fasted, alone; I wanted to see it for myself. I did 18/6 as much as possible, meaning a window of 6 hours of eating and about 18 hours of fasting. After three weeks, the cat was out of the bag: I had to explain myself and I experienced clashes between the traditional conversations of the conventional food guide and this method of intermittent fasting. The word "fasting" is scary. However, a loss of 17 pounds in 3 weeks validated my method and nothing could stop me. I was pumped and confident.

I knew that by the holiday season I would be back to being a "normal" person with a healthy weight; I felt it and I believed myself mentally strong enough to accomplish this feat. I had also promised myself to take all the possible medical exams towards the end of November, when I would have lost a ton of weight (so to speak), so as not to suffer any collateral problems and to have myself validated by the laboratories. Caution is required, of course. I don't know your medical condition, but in my case I was not taking any medication, I was ready to start and test this intermittent fasting according to my own method.

I was almost ready to comply with the pill prescriptions of my family doctor in the famous health care system used to cure us, which is different than a system to keep us healthy.

Skipping breakfast was easy, because during my many years in business, in my 20s and 30s, I started my days very early, under stress, and more often than not I didn't eat, being simply in too much of a hurry. Everything was in place to really try this new lifestyle with the advice of cardiologists who didn't want to sell me anything. I like listening to cardiologists who have nothing to sell or promote except a healthy life; this in literally striking logic.

Let's go in sequences, evolving from the first to the last of these activities that I loved doing and that I wanted to do again.

It is July 2023 and I estimated that in November I would be able to take my first physical and mental challenge, and test the condition of my leg as a basketball referee. It's been 30 years since I refereed and I've always loved basketball, but to run around a gym for 90 minutes with kids aged 14 to 18, you have to be able to follow the parade.

This was my first test. What will yours be? Create your goal to achieve and, whatever its nature, it will be yours.

It could be three minutes of chair yoga a day or a walk around the block, but write it down and aim for it. Then identify the next one and so on. Record your progress in writing because, you know too well, by losing weight you will cure all your other physical ailments; you will feel better. And as time goes by, the weight will drop, and the more you will be able to meet your challenges, ranging from the easiest to the most difficult.

I had noted hockey and skiing in my sequence of activities to return to. I was offered to join an old timer hockey league in Bromont, Qc. I refused because, at 300 pounds, the exercise of simply tying up your laces on your skates represents an adventure. The standard excuses saved me at the time, but now I thought that by December I might be ready to put on my skates and ski boots again. I bought the missing pieces of equipment and, without any problem, laced up my skates and jumped on the ice.

Even with my five years of experience skiing big Whistler mountains, I wanted to go to smaller Bromont ski hill to do a few descents, because the simple fact of going there, showing up, putting my skis on my shoulder, walking in ski boots to the lift chair is a victory. Skiing and hockey were my winter victories to validate the value of my new lifestyle; in other words, a return to the things that bring me joy. Find your second target in your journey and write it down.

It's not over. I want to aim far and progress, because I am alive and I feel good. At the age of 61, the simple fact of believing oneself capable brings strength and will. Spring, for me, will be a return to golf and, if all goes well, to competition, after an absence of around thirty years.

I reflected that when I performed best in competitive golf, it was when I was lean and flexible, while maintaining a healthy weight. This sequence of sports, for me, is not so much competitive as a simple personal challenge to be healthy. If I wanted to shine like before, I would have to bring my body back to the level of the good old days. I've done it confidently with intermittent fasting. Will I perform well? It's not that important, because my real victory is to have basically regained the same physical shape at 61 as at 21 and to give myself the chance to be physically ready for the challenge.

The result is secondary; it's the path to get there that matters most.

Dare to return to your past because you want to find this great forgotten physical form.

automne 1981 staff photo by Dale Omori

BG sophomore Jean LaRochelle follows through in yesterday's first round of the BG-UT Fall Golf Classic at the University Golf Course.

My last milestone is a crazy one for me. I had tried it only once, without success: doing real surfing in the ocean. This step is my last and it represents the achievement of my goals within the framework of this new lifestyle. Then, I will have to stay in shape, and I am confident of succeeding 100 %, because I now have full control of everything and all the tools. I don't depend on doctors, trainers, medications, nor pills; I simply have to follow my own guides, guides that I have established myself, for myself.

Why surf? Lying flat on your stomach on a board, popping up and standing up on your feet requires instant strength and abs ready for that one or two second leap. I was totally out of my comfort zone, and for a guy who grew up on golf courses, water sports don't come naturally at all. I decided to take this last step in November 2024, and I am constantly training for it.

I believe you must complete your steps. By the time you reach your final stage, your life will be so different that exciting new challenges will naturally present themselves. You have to aim far, but not too far. Be realistic, go about it in moderation with the aim of reaching your targets in one year.

MY CHOICE: You have seen my clearly detailed four-step chart.

YOUR REFLECTION: This is your first homework and your first step towards another world. Write down your steps, the ones that make you happy. Which ones are you planning for next year? Find them and name them in the correct sequence.

The evolution of man

Do you think humans were put on this planet by ordering a pizza over the phone, or even going to the drive-thru? Obviously not! Modern industrial agriculture is only 200 years old and the high consumption of sugar has been wreaking havoc for barely 150 years. So, what was happening 1000 years ago? The caveman was a hunter forced to fast while waiting for his new prey. He became vigilant and his body had to fuel on something else during periods of food shortage.

The human body has its built-in mechanisms that are useful during these periods without food; For thousands of years of evolution, the human machine has survived.

Fasting is really nothing new. It has only been forgotten because the lobbies of multinationals and our governments want to sell us more products instead of keeping us healthy. I invite you to reduce your expenses and let your body naturally generate its powers acquired over thousands of years of evolution.

Socrates fasted for clarity of mind, and followers of many religions have done so for various reasons for centuries. The concept is not new, but popular thinking tells us that if we don't eat, we will become weak and sleepy when, in fact, quite the opposite happens. Another free world awaits you on the other side of the darkness: go and discover it.

The human we know is old, in fact 2.5 million years old. Some 12,000 years ago, man changed his way of life: he began to practice agriculture. Before that, we were much more Paleolithic and we ate meat, some vegetables and fruit, and we drank a lot of water. And, meanwhile, none of our ancestors went hunting every three hours to eat all day with two snacks between meals. Over these thousands of years, humans have generated genetic diversity and we have the resulting genetics today. So, humans evolved and became more intelligent by developing their agriculture and, as a result, their food changed. Do you think that human genetics has followed the change of the last century and a half? No! Why?

It would take 2.5 million more years to establish these new modern sugar-filled genetics.

Over the years, the population increases and agriculture becomes more efficient in order to feed the masses. 200 years ago, we changed our diet again. Now we are industrialized, we eat processed and manufactured foods. As a result, our hormones and system are once again challenged by this new chemistry.

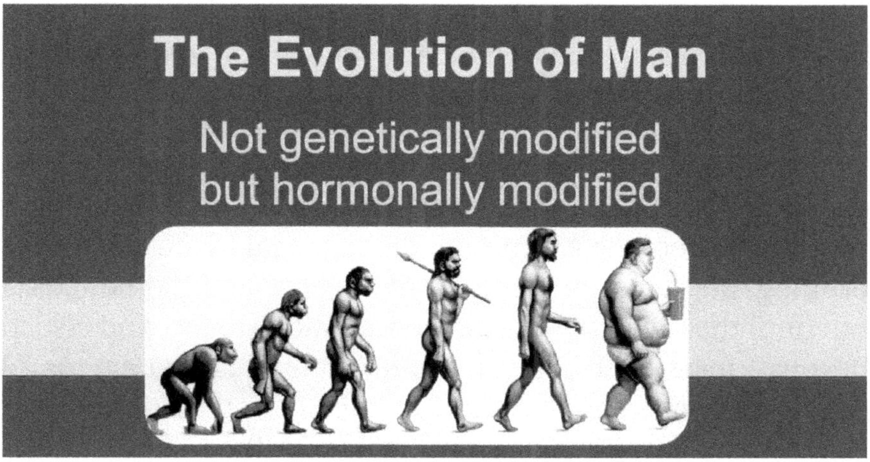

Vegetable oil is a "poison" manufactured for 200 years by companies who simply want our money and not our well-being. This oil requires tons of machines to produce and we find it everywhere, as if it were good for us. Why don't our governments tell us the truth? To ask the question is to answer it. They want us as customers, obviously, and we get hooked. The next time you have a food rage, ask yourself if your sugar levels are that low or if you are now addicted to junk food.

All products manufactured with sugar, vegetable oil and a long list of chemicals have the ability to make you addicted. This vegetable oil is found in all processed foods. Did you know that if you reheat fries cooked in vegetable oil in the microwave, you will create your own trans fat and a real poison? If we look at the evolution of humans over 12,000 years, how do you expect the human body to be able to adapt to this new ingredient manufactured by machines in such a short time?

Two centuries of man's great evolution are equivalent to one second of his history. We should ask ourselves the following question before eating: "Is this good for my genetics?". Agricultural products are healthy when they are prepared in the right way and in their pure state, but around 1880 we perfected the mills and the manufacture of flour. So, flour changed everything and screwed up our glycemic index.

As humans, we have changed over the last 200 years, but our body comes from another era.

Paleolithic man normally only ate once a day, when he could, and he did so in broad daylight, because he hid at night so as not to become another predator's meal of the day. In the evening, our ancestor returned to his cave and did not come out until the morning. Our bodies are made to fast and also to devour a feast: both. Do you think that if you don't eat for 24 hours, you will become weak, go back to your cave and die? No, fasting doesn't kill anyone; in fact, it's the food that kills.

When you are sick, your appetite decreases and you naturally fast. You don't eat because you instinctively want to cleanse your system. If your dog is sick, he will lie down, stay quiet and not eat. This wisdom comes from physiology, because imagine if you consumed 100 calories, your body would take another 60 just to digest them. We treat food as an activity, but we should instead consider that eating is dangerous.

MY CHOICE: I decided to refuse to eat when it is not the right time to do so. It doesn't matter what the situation is if I want to achieve my goal.

YOUR THOUGHT: Imagine yourself in a social or family context where you are offered food or drinks that fill you up even though you are not really hungry. Would you be able to turn it down?

Instead of using their body and its natural abilities, the human being of our century likes to consume energy bars or energy drinks to give themselves a false impression of renewed life. Wrong: in fact, we consume sugar and we become addicted to it. When you take one of these energizing products, you feel better and experience some pressure coming down; but do you know why? You are a junkie just like a hard drug addict, except sugar is your heroin.

You have generated a dose of dopamine with this energy product which goes directly to your brain to relieve you, to falsely reward you; but, unfortunately, you are addicted to sugar. In fact, there is no biochemical mechanism proving the consumption of these products gives you relief; none, scientifically speaking. It's all in the strength of the mind and you send a signal to your brain to validate this false relief. Yes, it's all mental.

It is also scientifically proven that a 48 hour fast acts as a reboot or a boost to your dopamine system and your satisfaction is gained through this fast, instead of sugar.

You have to be careful not to jump into a 48-hour fast too quickly. You must learn to walk before you run; take it gradually and I will discuss the different fasts in more depth later.

When you fast, you will feel a little weakness for a short period of time, while the body reacts to its lack of sugar and wants to draw on its fat reserves. Once you have gone through this period, you move on to the other side of your body's life, which runs on fat. Biomechanical reasoning explains this, but to fight the demons of addiction to sugar and other substances, you need treatment similar to that of an alcoholic or a drug addict who wants to get out of it, that is to say gradually. and one step at a time.

After a few days of abstinence, we can all get by, but we just want more when we're addicted. We must relentlessly fight these attacks of gluttony, these surges of dopamine. This battle is fought with will and an improved vision of life.

The other great enemy is the Pavlovian reflex which automates us in our lives.

We are conditioned to eat at a certain time in a certain place, every day: we follow the routine and the crowd.

If you have a break at 10 a.m. and you enjoy your snack, you do it without asking yourself any questions, like a programmed being; we follow the others. Are you hungry? "No, but I have to eat, because it's time to eat." In the evening, at home, you are used to eating while watching television, so without necessarily feeling hungry. You eat out of habit.

Is your stomach taking a break? We have simply stopped listening to our bodies and we follow this schedule which leads to all these beautiful modern diseases such as diabetes, hypertension, Alzheimer's, stroke, cardiovascular problems and cancer. Think about it, all of these diseases are part of a huge economy and various companies, including doctors, rely on you as a customer. Why would they advise you to consume half as much, at the risk of losing you as a customer and for the benefit of your perfect health? It's neither profitable nor sexy to consume nothing.

Why have we stopped listening to our bodies? Our brain interferes with our body and tells us to eat to feel good because, after all, what's better than a nice glass of wine and abundant food? We are told all our lives by the media, advertisements and even our close friends or family to eat well. It is a national value instilled in us at a young age. My late father, who died too young, at 70, often said: "The fork kills!" He had lived through the typical food generation of the time, but he knew very well what was happening without really understanding the whole concept of what he was saying.

Your biggest challenge is to listen to yourself, to stay the course while challenging those close to you, because you will have to explain yourself one day.

This does not mean not being present; this means that a meal may fall in a bad window of your fast. Nothing stops you from sitting down to join your group of friends with a glass of water for a laugh, because in the end you will be happier; quite simply. Additionally, your brain will be on and alert; you will be pleasantly surprised. Forget the famous food guide that programs you to eat constantly. In addition, now we add snacks between meals, as if humans would collapse or die without them.

Someone is making money off your belly, plain and simple! It's nothing new, money runs the world.

Breakfast is the most important meal of the day

False! Totally false! This rather ludicrous idea results from a slogan launched by an American cereal company during the

1960s. However, this principle established a persistent false mentality from which large corporations and governments still benefit today. We are sold on this idea, which we buy in as if they were words of gospel. The English word breakfast means break the fast. A renowned researcher from a major American university has concluded that we should never eat three hours before going to bed, nor one hour after getting up, regardless of our lifestyle. If you snack in the evening while watching TV, you need to stop now, because your digestion and stomach need a rest; quite simply.

I sense you are curious and you are asking me which meal is the most important, if it is not breakfast. Here is my answer: "The one you are currently having."

When a multinational company wants to develop a special breakfast product for you, expect to consume sugar, a product identified by a barcode and manufactured using machines, a bit like dog meat. Who are you going to believe between these capitalist companies interested in selling you more products, or cardiologists with nothing to sell? You really don't need all of these products for breakfast and the caveman survived centuries without eating them. Like it or not, we are all descended from cavemen. However, he did not consume sugary cereals accompanied by a glass of artificially sweetened orange juice.

MY CHOICE: I decided it was easy for me to skip breakfast, to give my stomach a needed break and cut morning calories, after having done it often in my entrepreneurial career to save time.

YOUR REFLECTION: Ask yourself if you would be able to give up a meal, ideally breakfast or dinner. Which one would be better for you to skip?

Is breakfast really the most important meal of the day?

No ! The most important meal is the one you are having !

The biochemistry of the body

The body has the natural ability to manage food. For 12 hours, it will consume the glycogen that exists in your liver and in your muscles; it uses sugar to move forward. After these 12 hours, depending on what you consumed the day before, the body will enter the other paying zone, that is to say it will fuel itself with fat, normally after 13 or 14 hours of fasting. I assure you that I felt all of this and that I still feel it today, because fasting creates a sensation in the body, captured or experienced cerebrally. The body has reserves of proteins and vitamins for 30 days; fat for 40 days. In addition, it processes some 50,000 calories stored in its tissues.

The key is to unlock this fat reserve and draw from it what is necessary during a fast in order to function. This operation aims directly to help you lose weight, in addition to allowing you to have clarity of mind and to completely renew your weak cells, even cancerous ones. The benefits of fasting are widely documented by science, but who is going to promote the consumption of nothing?

How will you feel when you reach the 13th hour of fasting? You'll be perfect, unless you're a modern-day sugar addict. I felt a little bad the first two days after this change in lifestyle, because I felt my stomach rumbling. I wanted to persist and really see this project through to the end and I thank my inner strength for that. There's no denying it, you have to change certain aspects of your life if you want changes. Quite logical: don't change anything, nothing will change. Don't try anything and nothing will happen to you.

It is up to you to decide your final destination and to set milestones and goals. I told you about mine, which you could use as inspiration to establish your own, your own steps and objectives. Every person is different. There is no one mold fits all model. Take control and rush into your own mold, which is based on the history of human beings, the same humans who have survived thousands of years.

You can medically fast for seven days without experiencing a hypoglycemic crisis: your sugar level will drop, but you will survive. I must tell you my personal preferences, because after all I advocate custom made adaptations of this lifestyle regimen. I advise you to build your own diet; but so far, mine has not yet exceeded 72 hours. Additionally, I only made it to this 72 hour stage a few times. I stay more inside the range between two meals a day, up to 48 hours of fasting, to just one meal a day; or 36 hours of fasting, my favorite duration of fasting.

Why? Because the body gets used to everything and if you always do the same thing, it becomes regulated and you will quickly reach plateaus.

Why do you think traditional diets don't work? You follow a recipe prescribed by our product suppliers and service companies; you are fighting an already lost war. Your body can lower its metabolism and adapt to your diet changes. The worst mistake is to always do the same thing, day after day. In my hundreds of hours of research, I discovered that those who fasted for long periods, beyond 7 days, up to 30 days even, all shared the same disappointment in the end: they all found that 'They should have lost more weight."

Again, the body adapts and gets used to even fasting, and the key is to not follow the same routine day after day. Do you think that our ancestor, the caveman, had his own eating routine? We come from him, however; our genetics and our DNA have a history that must be taken into account.

Your sugar levels will never drop if you eat constantly. Many people fuel themselves with sugar throughout their entire lives, without having ever used the other fuel stored in the form of fat in their body. What happens if you don't eat anything? Your body will absorb the proteins that are already in it, but they are not muscle proteins. Your metabolism begins by going into a state of ketosis. How? The body senses that no food is coming in, and it's not just about sugar. Suddenly, your body sees its insulin level drop and it must draw its energy from what is available: fat.

Conversely, when your insulin level is high, you store energy in the form of fat and the best place to put this fat is your stomach. Around the 18th hour of fasting, ketone usage begins and gradually increases, and by the 24th hour of abstinence, your body is functioning at around 15% on these natural ketones. During this ketosis, your fatty acids go to the liver and are transformed into energy. These same ketones can be used by every cell in your body, including those in your brain.

We are so programmed to eat to make us feel better and to think that our brain only works with sugar and food consumption... This is totally false. The brain likes to feed itself on this fuel during fasting and a study shows that after seven days of fasting, the brain functions 70% on ketones. I am not suggesting that you fast for seven days in a row right away, but this principle is palpable from the first moments of a fast of a few hours. How do you feel when you're running on your ketones? Perfectly, because these ketones provide you with the energy you need to properly function and you have unparalleled mental clarity. You only drink water, black coffee or herbal tea, nothing else.

However, for a complete detoxification, it is best to avoid coffee but I like coffee, so I keep drinking it. There are many electrolytes on the market to help the body, and some are flavored to enhance the taste; so, I now like to add it to my water. Now go beyond 24 hours and stretch to 36 hours: those ketone levels go into another pay zone and you have to remember not to repeat the same thing day after day.

Many opt for a 36-hour fast per week and do not change their diet the rest of the time, but monitor the quality of the products they consume, and they obtain excellent results. Everyone finds what they're looking for in their own way, quite simply. Ketone levels are easily measured with urine, but I have never done it. I rely more on my feeling. I am following my new lifestyle all by myself, I am doing it my way and I want to rely more on my own sensations than on measured data. It's up to everyone to make their choices.

If you eat fewer carbs and less sugar, you reach the state of ketosis much faster than someone who eats poorly and fills up on glycogen and sugar. You should always keep in mind that your body must burn all its sugar reserves before falling into ketosis. Therefore, a healthy diet is the key to success, because there is no magic. Fasting while continuing to eat poutines, fried foods and sweets every day makes no sense.

If you don't want to change your eating habits, don't start a fast, because how you break the fast is as important as the fast itself.

MY CHOICE: When I started this lifestyle regimen, I wrote down the non-negotiable foods that I like to eat and the bad ones that I could live without.

YOUR REFLECTION: Consider the importance of breaking your fast with natural foods that you love. Which ones?

Add electrolytes to your water and it will bring you sodium, magnesium, potassium and more.

Fasting produces less insulin naturally

Our body fuels like a hybrid car: it runs on either sugar or fat. When you combine natural, non-manufactured foods and bring your body into ketosis, you see instant, easy-to-repeat results. Suddenly you think it's easy! Quickly you have full control like you've never had before. However, you should not repeat the same recipe every day like a programmed zombie; in fact, you have to vary and break the routine. A pizza night, why not? A good spaghetti or even a sloppy poutine, why not?

It is not about living inside a sect which multiplies strict rules; it is a healthy lifestyle. But don't overdo it.

Your insulin is the key that opens fat cells. If you want to eat fat, insulin production must decrease. Therefore eating healthy and drinking well is essential. There is only one way to lower this insulin level: fasting. It all happens in fasting, with insulin, and anyone who injects it is somewhat doomed right out of the gate. In type 2 diabetics, the insulin level is high and they are given more insulin to get a lower number, but nothing that will help them live longer or avoid heart attacks, strokes, etc. To my knowledge, no medication can lower your insulin levels; only fasting achieves this feat.

When your insulin level drops, you become receptive to other new insulin, and vice versa if you have too much. So during your next meal following a 24-hour fast, for example, you will produce less insulin with that meal; it is scientifically proven. Under the effect of fasting, your body reacts differently to your next meal, compared to its reaction to the three meals a day recommended by the food guide. For a single day of fasting, your body will produce less insulin than during days with regular meals.

Imagine the free benefits of just one day of fasting per week: your ability to produce insulin will greatly improve.

What are the different types of fasting?

There are several ways to fast and you will need to find the one that seems best for you. Additionally, changing the way you fast along the way and switching between methods as needed is highly recommended. Some fast every other day, others for 24 hours straight, while others for 36 hours. Many stick to 14 to 18 hours of fasting per day and get excellent results.

You are asking me why we couldn't eat small quantities five times a day? Your metabolism would drop, you'd feel crooked, and worst of all, your body would reset and you'd gain the lost weight back in a split second. It's just not natural to eat that often and, again, imagine your caveman ancestor: he didn't eat five times a day. So why would you do it? We're all descended from that troglodyte, aren't we? In reality, we are only supposed to eat once a day, when food is available. As simple as that!

I love the slogan "Feast and fast". It sums it all up perfectly. We were programmed to eat when we had just hunted our food, and then fast until the next kill and feast again.

MY CHOICE: I decided to vary my fasts during my week by trying to include a 36-hour fast and possibly 2 or 3 other 24-hour days.

YOUR REFLECTION: Imagine what would be achievable according to your courage and your initial conviction... Wouldn't it be to start with 16 hours of fasting? You need to start slowly and increase gradually.

The many benefits of fasting

What are the other benefits of fasting? Your body, after an 18-hour fast, tells itself that it hasn't had any food because you haven't found your next prey. So in its own right, it increases your metabolic rate to help you hunt. Your adrenaline increases, so does your cortisol level; you are alert, turned on and alive. Think about it: given that humans have been able to survive for thousands of years, logically they had to be turned on to find their next prey. This mechanism sleeps inside us, and with free access.

If the caveman had slept or lacked strength while fasting, we wouldn't be here today talking about it, because natural selection would have eliminated us long ago. So, you are on alert to hunt your next meal, with a sharp mind in survival mode.

Another important factor in a fasting state: your body produces a hormone that goes to your brain, turns on the "circuit breaker" and produces new cells, no less. Find me a drug that can produce new brain cells! It's a way for your body to learn and become smarter. "And now get moving and go hunt for something to eat!" In short, fasting improves your brain; as simple as that.

What else? Fasting produces growth hormones that would cost thousands of dollars if injected. It is scientifically proven that a 48-hour fast produces 2000% more growth hormones in men. Fasting is the best way to increase your growth hormones, and you will probably wonder why I would want growth hormones. The answer is simple. Growth hormones keep you young, improve your skin, replace dead cells, and allow your muscles to grow bigger and respond better to physical activity. To gain muscle, you need growth hormones.

Autophagy

What else? In one word: autophagy. This self-digestion process is a way for your body to renew old cells, recycling damaged proteins. Consider backwashing filters in your pool: we remove the dirt and sand and keep the water clean. This process in humans begins after 18 hours of fasting and reaches its maximum effect after 3 days of fasting.

Autophagy is a process that transforms your old cells and reuses them as fuel; it cleans your system at the same time. You recycle yourself. And when you eat, you will nourish affected cells, which results in a form of rejuvenation.

Therefore, if you eat constantly you never recycle these cells and nutrients pile up on your cells; result: your intestine becomes irritable, or inflamed. When our cells are cleaned through autophagy, they recycle, get stronger, last longer and are more resistant to disease. Autophagy is like "turning on a circuit breaker" in your body and your cells become alert and intelligent. Caution: however, let's avoid chronic fasting, which would inhibit the function of autophagy and could lead to neuronal damage.

After this recycling, the bone marrow sends the new nutrients from the next meal to these cells in need, and thereby creates stem cells. The medical industry sells stem cells for millions of dollars, even though they are naturally free. Why doesn't anyone recommend these methods to you? Because they don't bring in a penny! In addition, artificial stem cell injections only work very little despite their exorbitant cost.

Fasting is the fastest way to obtain real stem cells naturally.

303 lb

303 lb

302 lb

300 lb

290 lb

You become a better person, healthier, more resilient, more resistant to disease... All of this is well documented by researchers and those who are willing to promote staying healthy instead of curing diseases. It is much more profitable, financially, to write prescriptions to cure illnesses than to promote the preservation of health by selling nothing. Who will benefit financially if you live longer and feel better and healthier?

A study from Boston showed that if you fast for seven days, your risk of cancer is reduced by 70 %, because cancer cells die. Another study on cancer and fasting shows that a patient who fasted 36 hours before receiving chemotherapy treatment will tolerate their treatment better. It will have fewer side effects and its normal cells will be more resistant.

When you fast, your cells become stronger and chemotherapy only kills weak cancer cells; so the stronger your cells are, the better you are. But in medical reality, this is not possible: we continue to feed patients, we make them feel nauseous and then prescribe them all kinds of medications. We want to create a domino effect, making you fall into the vicious cycle of remedies, in the need to see a doctor, and you wake up one morning taking six pills a day.

What's more, autoimmune diseases and diabetes can be relieved by fasting because your stomach and digestive system have time to rest and not work for a period of time.

Want more? Not feeding our elders and making them fast, instead of bringing them trays of food like in a manufacturing plant, has been proven to help them fight Alzheimer's disease and dementia. Taking such an action for the benefit of our elderly would be seen as a crime against humanity; so be prepared to get arrested by the police, because we are so programmed to eat throughout our society that the opposite is practically illegal.

In fact, Grandma could follow a three-day fast and come out in better shape, with instant visible improvements. Alas we don't do it! Our health system is incompatible with the practice of fasting.

Drink plenty of water

A real fast is done by drinking only water. You'll want to urinate regularly, because when your insulin level goes down, that insulin holds onto water; hence the water flow navigates more easily throughout your body.

You should drink more water when you fast. It is even the best way to combat an increase in hunger, and it is at that very moment that you must draw on your unwavering will in order to achieve the desired goal.

Resist and drink a large glass of water, and 15 minutes later you will be "normal" again. This buffer zone exists. For my part, I add a pack of electrolytes from time to time and I continue to fast normally without any problem. Another method is to add a little salt to your glass of water; we suggest Himalayan pink salt. This improves your endurance, decreases the chances of cramps, dizziness and headaches, in addition to regulating the sodium level in your system. If you have a slight headache, simply drink more water and add a little salt or a packet of electrolyte powder.

Dizziness normally results from a drop in blood pressure when your sugar levels drop. Drink water, and all you need is salt and magnesium. Are you hungry? I understand. Tell yourself that hunger comes and goes, because it follows a cycle... especially at the beginning. Personally, I had to make an effort not to break my fast, but, depending on the activity of the moment, I managed to get through it and, a few minutes later, completely forget that I had been hungry.

Stay busy, do an activity, get moving and keep your mind active. Hunger will slowly fade away on its own. The first two days are always the hardest; afterward, everything becomes easier. Patients who are in the clinic to do fasts adopt this mold during the first two days, which are the most difficult. Once they reach the fourth or fifth day, they feel full of vigor and they all want to do sports activities.

The ultimate goal is to eat once or twice a day within a 6-hour window, with 18 hours of fasting. You will notice a noticeable difference in your health and your daily life.

The most popular formula is as follows: lunch around noon and dinner around 6 p.m.; the rest of the time, you fast by drinking only water. No more snacking between meals in the false belief that it gives you strength. Ultimately, you're going to get a little bit of autophagy, a little bit of ketosis, and you're going to burn fat. Your body will get used to this new cycle that you won't find in any governmental food guide.

You could stretch this out to once a week by skipping the morning or evening meal, to complete 24 hours of fasting and that's it. Your immunity rate will improve because your stem cells are awake and active. The most rewarding fast is the 36 hour fast and, honestly, I've done it several times without any problems.

MY CHOICE: When I feel suddenly hungry, I drink two good glasses of water, to which I sometimes add a pack of electrolytes or a little Himalayan salt.

YOUR REFLECTION: During your first days of fasting, you will have to deal with hunger. Will your inner strength to achieve your goal be strong enough to resist this temporary hunger?

Beliefs

With our modern lives flooded by the food industry, media and governments, we are lost in associating eating with happiness. Eating can kill you; but not fasting. By fasting, naturally, antioxidant genes are generated. So you don't need to go out and buy supplements and vitamins of all kinds. Simply get rid of what has been in your body for thousands of years. In the worst of all worlds, my good doctors suggest vitamin D, because it affects the expression of your genetics and every meal you eat affects it. It is said that 90% of the population lacks vitamin D. Therefore, take your vitamin D3 and go out and catch a few rays for 10 minutes a day.

Fruit is so overrated! As if we had to listen to government authorities to guide us in our lives... I learned that we should eat a maximum of one fruit per day and choose one with a low sugar level. Think about it for two seconds: we give it to animals before winter for their energy supply during this period, while we consume it 12 months a year with our eyes closed. Try to choose colorful fruits. Sugar causes inflammation in the body and fructose, which is a form of sugar produced by fruit, causes insulin resistance in the liver. Industrial sugar is poison. It does not come from nature: it is completely manufactured by man and his machines.

Another concept poorly evaluated by the general population is the consumption of proteins. Yes! Don't think I don't eat any. In fact, I probably consume too much. When I told you that everyone must create their own lifestyle regimen and that you must adapt it according to your preferences, I choose to eat more protein than my good doctors suggest: around one gram per pound of weight. If I weigh 200 pounds, I get 200 grams of protein, and if I eat a good steak or spaghetti sauce, I am sorry but I don't count. I eat it and even often... I spoil myself. I mentally think about the theory "feast and fast", and I believe in feasting too.

Stuffing yourself into a treat a few times gives your body a better chance to bounce back afterward and lose weight, even break through the inevitable plateaus.

I know I'm repeating myself, but you shouldn't do the same thing every day. According to my good doctors, do not take animal protein powder because, think about it, you are no longer growing. You're probably not a bodybuilder, you are past puberty, and these artificial concoctions contain glucose, decrease autophagy, and increase cancer risks. I described autophagy to you and often these protein mixtures turn off autophagy; so you prevent your body from recycling its old, useless cells. Do you want good protein? Eat a good lean chicken or turkey or fish instead of man-made powder.

In my 30s, I wanted to lose weight, and I consulted a registered dietitian who advised me I could eat as much meat as I wanted. Yes, a buffet, eat by the ton and lose weight. (I'm being ironic.)

255 lb

228 lb

216 lb

217 lb

202 lb

195 lb

195 lb

188 lb

185 lb

Obviously, that didn't work and she then advised me to do 20 minutes of stationary cycling to improve my chances, as she earns her living within a (nutrition) system where the client loses before even starting; this while the consultant collects his or her hard earned money. Professionals want to see you again and again, to sell another service. Someone, somewhere wants to sell you products; rest assured. I want to help you save on your grocery bills and any medical expenses that may arise. Who are you going to believe?

It's not going to happen tomorrow

How many generations do you think have gone before us? For 2.5 million years, 100,000 generations of humans have survived before us, including Homo sapiens who appeared 200,000 years ago, and now modern man. With natural selection and the passing of centuries, each generation improves its genetics. Otherwise, we wouldn't be here. Agriculture only affected the last 600 of these 100,000 generations, and this old agriculture was still decent with grains and other products.

But only 10 generations lived in the industrial era. Yes, only the last 10 out of 100,000 generations of our human species. So, how do you think our famous way of living can be compatible with our genetics? Impossible! Modern humans are in a phase of extreme hormonal change and we find ourselves with all the known medical problems and an epidemic of obesity.

Today we are doomed. We have no chance of getting out of this one, no chance. Look at the society around you, which reflects our life choices. Man makes drastic diet changes and thinks that his genetics will adapt through the timely intervention of the Holy Spirit, when we know full well that our future children, to adapt to the toxic products that we consume without hesitation think twice, would need 1000 generations to absorb such a change in food consumption.

Yes, 1000 generations will be necessary. So, it is not tomorrow that the new generation will adapt to this new menu full of sugar, vegetable oil and manufactured products, because for humans this menu is really new.

If you decide instead to give this lifestyle regimen that includes fasting a chance, the first thing to do is to take it gradually, slowly and cut out carbohydrates and as much man-made food as possible. Also, cut out anything sweet, all juices and carbonated drinks. Drink only water. This seems exaggerated to you, but you have to choose: either you continue what you are currently doing or change and take charge of yourself. Tea or coffee is permitted during your fasts, but without adding anything to it; I like black coffee without sugar, milk or cream.

My good doctors praise the benefits of black coffee on the system and, according to my personal analysis, caffeine promotes a renewed life and is beneficial when taken in moderation. I also add MCT oil (modular source of medium chain triglycerides) to my first coffee. As this oil helps to calm hunger, I recommend it. The list of products that I suggest and that I consume myself is very short and inexpensive (MCT oil and electrolytes); much shorter than those of grocery stores that I will spare you, which can amount to thousands of dollars annually. I had to get rid of my entire wardrobe; the money saved on my grocery bills was used to buy size 34 waist clothes, along with size large shirts; no more XXXL and size 44.

Obviously, I buy fewer groceries and waste a lot less, which means I save a lot of money while improving my health and quality of life. ***What can be better?***

During fasting, add a teaspoon of MCT oil to help you resist those cravings and to give you energy.

How to break the fast is as important as the fast

Breaking your fast is super important. Simply fasting is not a solution and if you don't make the other right choices, it can even become dangerous. How you break your fast is as important as the fast itself. My good doctors preach homemade bone broth as the best way, unequivocally. Some even say that you can even take it if you ever have a hunger crave during a fast; but a homemade broth in preference to a manufactured concoction.

Personally, I tried to do it and I had organizational problems. I'm not exactly a great chef, and the flavor wasn't exactly there. There are good quality bone broths available now and I like them. If everyone needs to create their own custom diet, I chose boiled eggs, turkey, tuna and my favorite vegetables. It seems to work wonderfully.

Don't think that you will be able to enjoy poutine, a good piece of toast spread with industrial peanut butter or other junk every time you break your fast, because you will feel bad pretty quickly.

In fact, as you navigate this lifestyle, your taste develops and you learn the effect of certain foods on your body. The more time passes, the more natural and easier your choice to eat well becomes, because you feel the benefits of eating well, without taking into account the harmful effects of bad choices. In short, when you think about it, the choice is in front of you: after having tasted both worlds, you will choose that of intermittent fasting. I guarantee it.

Play the monkey

Calories go hand in hand with diseases. The more calories you eat, the more diseases you attract; It's quite simple thank you. I am aware of a serious study done on monkeys. These primates are still quite close to us in terms of evolution. We created two groups: we fed the first with our modern products of sugars, oils, etc., without restriction. For the second group, we simply reduced the number of calories by 30%; nothing else. This study lasted three years and, at the end, members of the group who had reduced their calorie level by 30% lived 25% longer, had 50% fewer cardiovascular problems and over 90% less. between them showed no trace of diabetes. All these benefits obtained simply by reducing their calorie consumption by 30%.

Then, we conducted another study with the group which cut its calories by 30%, but this time the other controlled group ingested foods with the following characteristics: vegetable proteins, no animal proteins with the exception of fish, 5% fat, 4% sugar; the monkeys in this group were fed only twice a day. Which of these two groups do you think performed better? Of course, the group that ate twice a day was much more effective than the other, demonstrating that cutting calories is not the only answer; you have to eat the right foods at the right time. This demonstrates that calorie restricted diets have little lasting success, and are a false belief based on the number of calories you take in and spend. It's much more about how your body responds through your hormones and genetic code. We must be vigilant with what enters our body, because it will determine our future.

Harmful Foods To Eliminate

While you're thinking about trying a variation of fasting and reducing your window of time for eating, start by eliminating anything with sugar and, trust me, you're still going to eat some because sugar is simply everywhere. Nevertheless, it is a good first initiative to take. Next, remove the vegetable oils. I would go so far as to say that we should give up all oils except olive oil, coconut oil and avocado oil. You must take these actions if you want to see improvements, because the most important element in a fast is how to break it.

Imagine the caveman many centuries ago: after he had finished his feast, he must have cooked his leftover bones over the fire and drank the extracted juice as bone broth. The number one poison enemy is sugar, followed by vegetable oils. Then start pushing back your breakfast gradually by 30 minutes or an hour and I guarantee that these actions alone will give you amazing results.

Our number one enemy: sugar

Where does sugar come from? It dates back to the 12th century, and when sugar arrived in India around 1400, it was discovered that it could be reduced to particles without an expiration date; From then on, it can be transported and sold anywhere around the world. So, in our entire history, sugar hasn't been around for long, but its impact is devastating. It is only during wars that its consumption stagnates; the rest of the time, sugar is constantly increasing to make us totally dependent and addicted.

On a global scale, you'll hear about a population in a given location that eats carbs and is healthy. Then, on the other side of the world, another population eats only fish and is healthy. Another population, in another corner of the planet, eats something else and is also in perfect health. How can we navigate all of this? And who is right? You just have to look at what all these healthy people aren't eating: manufactured carbohydrates and sugar. We must eliminate the poisons before any further action. This is the priority.

Diabetes is the main cause of cardiovascular diseases. In fact, it should be considered a cardiovascular disease. Eliminate sugar right away before you fall victim to the unhealthy eating habits of modern man.

World Sugar Production

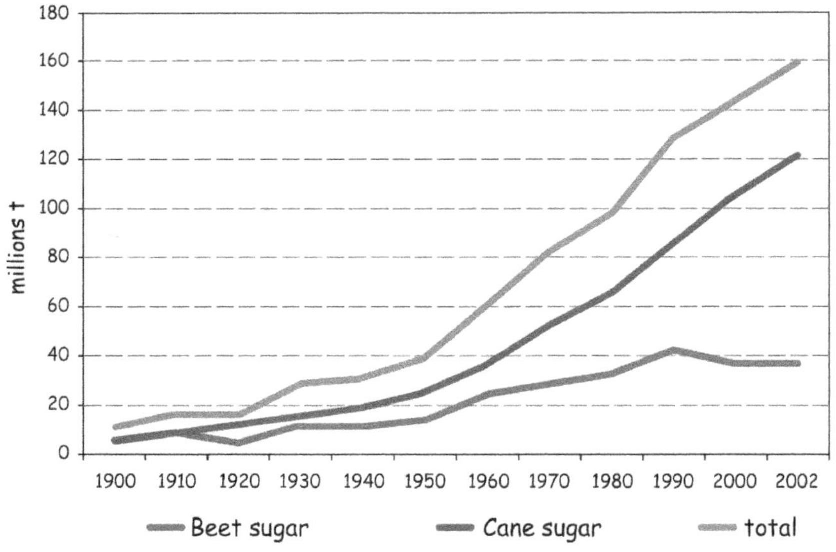

A bad diet with sugar will block your arteries. Your arteries are the perfect tracer to gauge whether you are old or young, instead of how many years you have been on earth.

You have unobstructed and functional arteries, you are young; otherwise, you're about to leave the planet... The toxic foods we all know make us insulin resistant. You also need to understand that in a state of fasting, you are actually in the natural human state, exactly where it should be. Humans are not made to eat all day, day after day, nor to eat the same menu at the same times every day. So if you eliminate these bad foods before fasting, your transition to burning energy through fat will be faster because you're eating right.

With a healthy diet, your sugar levels are lower and easier to switch to the other side to burn fat. Fasting is like sleeping, it is your natural healer. You must create the optimal conditions so that your body has the ability to draw on fat for fuel, and for this, you must prepare it with a conducive diet and healthier eating habits.

US Sugar Comsumption, 1822-2005

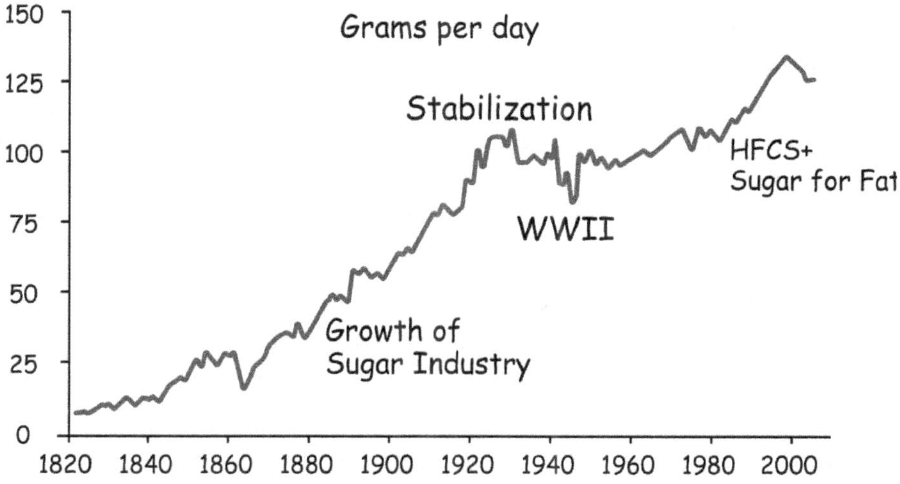

Traditional diets

How can we explain that the world we know today is debating the choice of the best diet, when no one is talking about fueling our body with stored fat? Why? You probably guessed it: nobody profits if you don't consume anything.

We never talk about the free healing that awaits us on the other side with fasting. In fact, we have a health system to cure diseases and but not to keep us healthy.

None of these calorie restricted diets work. None, unless you spend hours doing cardio every day and cut calories left and right. Unfortunately, your metabolism will get used to it and will set its new benchmark lower in order to make you regain the lost weight. All these diets will certainly make you lose some weight at first, but they will make you feel miserable, work you out and stress you out; they will make you lose muscle mass. To your great misfortune, your hormones will be as they were at the beginning, and you will quickly regain all that lost weight. But if you fast, you change your hormones, even your growth hormones, and you create autophagy, which is a recycling of your cells.

By fasting you lose weight during a hormonally altered condition and you will lose weight in the right places. You reshape your entire body naturally.

When you lose this weight thanks to fasting, your skin will not hang as much under your arms: you will be resculpted. Those who cut out all fat and reduce their carbohydrate intake to a minimum become miserable, depressed, and best of all, they no longer lose weight. The worst shortcoming of many diets is the fact that if we simply changed the window of time for eating by a setting of six or eight hours, without changing anything else, the body would have a better chance of resting and going in ketosis. But known traditional diets do none of this. Eat more and eat again; we even suggest snacks between meals.

Today, after months of practicing this lifestyle, I want to voluntarily fast, because I know that my clarity of mind will be there and that I will be alert to distinguish myself in my subjects of interest. In my ideal world, I like to go to do yoga around 10 a.m., on an empty stomach, and then I can decide whether I'm going to have lunch or fast straight to dinner; or, why not go the next morning for a good 36 hours of fasting?

Don't worry about being weak if you don't eat; this is false. It's actually quite the opposite. Of course, it will take a few weeks of implementation to understand it, when you have reached a certain cruising speed. You will have to draw on your willpower and get through the first two days. Then, through a gradual progression, you will discover a hidden and unknown universe which is buried in your body, freely offered by Mother Nature, who has been refining her work for thousands of years.

Fasting for women

There is no doubt, fasting is different for women, with three different phases. Dr. Mindy Pelz, who specializes in women's fasting, has written books on the subject and delivered multiple conferences. I will try to summarize the obvious differences from a hormonal point of view, based on the findings of this great expert.

If fasting gives excellent results for women before the start of their menstrual cycle thanks to estrogen, it is less efficient afterward, because of progesterone. Fasting after menstruation should be avoided, although there are nuances to this statement. In addition, women must look at their own lifestyle with a completely different eye and they cannot follow the same fasting method day after day, because the mechanics of female hormones are constantly changing.

Once again, we return to our caveman history. Back then, the women also spent days without food and had to pick fruits to eat, while the man hunted. This means that the expression fast and feast also applies to women. With that said, this rule is even more crucial for women, because they have two types of hormones: estrogen, which works very well with fasting, and progesterone, which does not cope very well with it.

By fasting, women will completely lower their progesterone levels. Therefore, if the woman is satisfied with one meal a day, she is likely to become anxious and not sleep well. What's more, her hair may start to fall out and she will have difficulty remaining calm.

The man functions mainly on testosterone; he receives a dose every 15 to 20 minutes. Estrogen levels are a negligible factor in men, because their testosterone cycle lasts about 24 hours. On the other hand, women have three hormones: progesterone, estrogen and testosterone, which are part of a cycle of 28 to 30 days. Testosterone performs wonderfully for both sexes in fasting, but women only receive testosterone during ovulation.

Sorry, I know it's totally unfair, men obtain superior results more easily when fasting than women, thanks to testosterone.

The two hormones, estrogen (before menstruation) and progesterone (after), must be treated differently. Let's start with estrogen, which is very forgiving: the woman can perform several physical or other tasks, including longer fasts and eating fewer carbohydrates. No matter what you do to lower your sugar levels so you can stock up on fat, estrogen is still going to be a holy beast. When we talk about progesterone, it's quite the opposite. It is therefore not suggested that women run a marathon on the 21st day of the menstrual cycle. When the cortisol level rises, the progesterone level drops and dries up; therefore, any form of stress or fasting will affect this hormone.

Another factor for a woman to consider is her insulin resistance during the week before her period. This benefits progesterone, which requires a high glucose level. Insulin resistance means that your cells cannot take advantage of insulin to your advantage, and your body will store glucose in fat or in the liver. (The liver converts glucose into glycogen for storage.) The opposite is being receptive to insulin, and in that case, your system uses the insulin and pushes the glucose into your mitochondria to use as an energy source.

According to several experts consulted, women must find a way to stabilize their sugar levels before even starting to fast. She must also increase her consumption of good fats which will stabilize her sugar levels. Conversely, bad fats will make you resistant to insulin. Fat is not the enemy: you have to choose the right fats, such as the right oils like MCT. When a woman stabilizes her sugar with the proper fat, the day following her fasting day is both easier and more productive.

Phase 1: fertility, normally 40 years and younger

During their fertile period, women are more resistant to insulin, lose their sensitivity to insulin, and therefore will experience a reduction in the uptake of sugar (glucose) by target cells. Normally, women want to binge eat and not do much during the week before their period. Chocolate cravings are in full swing, and everything is in place so that progesterone is well served, with an increasing glucose level. In general, women complain of premenstrual symptoms due to a lack of knowledge of their own body, as well as the balance necessary to control it well. Instead of diving into a pizza or a bag of candy, she should experiment with natural carbohydrates such as sweet potato. Women must certainly accept these changes, but they must also adapt by consuming more natural products, which will make fasting easier for better health.

Phase 2: premenopause and menopause, from 40 to 55 years old

This period is unique and each woman must find her own rhythm. Around age 40, the ovaries retire; they will take 10 or 15 years to complete this retirement. This is a slow descent of hormones. It is crucial for these women to know their cycle well, because you should not attack a three-day fast while the hormones are in full swing.

So, you need to know when estrogen is present. If it is day 10, the woman is ready for a fast. On the other hand, on day 22, progesterone (produced by the ovaries) is present even if the production of this hormone gradually reduces and will never be as high as in the twenties. The woman must juggle this information and know her cycle as much as possible, in order to avoid panic attacks and mood changes; because stress and fasting do not go well together. There is also a danger of weight gain; especially since standard diets tend not to work. In the end, if the woman practices fasting at the right time, she will obtain good results.

Phase 3: postmenopause, over 55 years old

At this stage of life, women no longer have a cycle to monitor or manage, but they still have three sex hormones, which are declining every day of their lives. So, they can experiment with different kinds of fasting, various diets; this can range from the keto diet to foods that help support hormones.

These women still have hormones racing through their bodies, but because their cycles have faded, they can now fast virtually at will. Consider adding fermented foods and probiotics, and reduce toxins, as well as beauty products applied to the skin, which may contain harmful toxins.

General conclusion for the woman: she must find her own fasting lifestyle and must deal with her hormonal changes throughout the years which go by too quickly.

In summary

The woman must find her niche, a lasting niche. The first 10 days of the menstrual cycle are ideal for fasting and balancing estrogen levels, while in the following five days, during ovulation, testosterone invades the woman, along with a little progesterone. Result: she finds herself with these three hormones at the same time. So, during ovulation, fasting should be reduced to around 15 hours maximum. Instead, women should eat better, especially vegetables, especially bitter ones, such as radicchio (red chicory). These vegetables will help your liver and stomach.

At the end of ovulation, around day 16, you have a period during which you can fast more than during ovulation; This window remains a good time to lose weight using 36-hour fasts.

The week of menstruation follows, around days 19 or 20. Progesterone levels rise and this hormone plays a different game: it will tease your psyche and make you crave chocolate and carbohydrates. This progesterone signals you to spike your sugar levels and sit on the couch doing nothing. In a simple formula, a woman's more stubborn hunger signals that progesterone is acting up; when the woman is less hungry, estrogen dominates.

Add MCT oil to your black coffee and as ketones rise to the brain, your hunger will decrease. I can validate this point, because I too add a little oil to my morning coffee. Also, add a pack of electrolytes to your water: this stuff tricks your brain into making your body fast more easily. The real battle in fasting – I would add in life in general – is in your head. The main battle rests on the strength of your mind.

Positife Effects of Fasting on Your Health

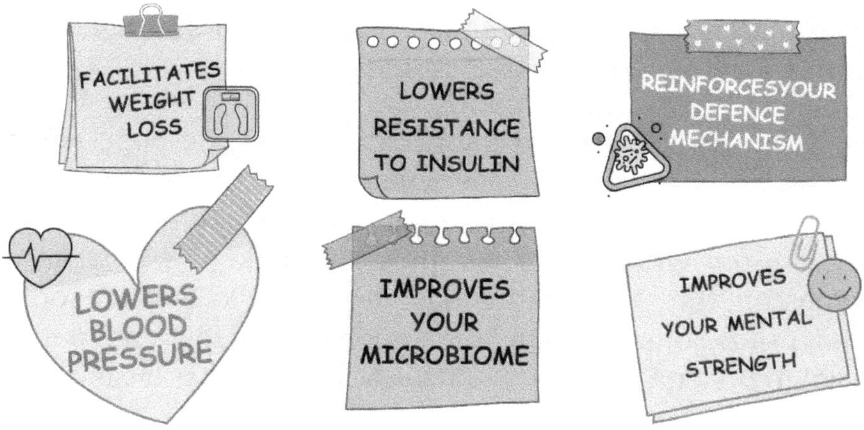

What to do if you reach a plateau?

No matter who you are or how you lose weight, you're going to hit a plateau at some point, with a good chance of feeling a little frustrated. By 2005, I had lost 70 pounds, was active and eating relatively well, knowing nothing about intermittent fasting, and an unbreakable plateau appeared when I weighed 235 pounds.

I wanted to lose more but I couldn't, until I followed this new intermittent fasting lifestyle plan, in 2023, with a weight of 202 pounds just 7 months later. In 2005 I couldn't understand why. I believed I was condemned to stagnate at 235 pounds, on the condition of perpetuating my lifestyle at the time (because you must always take into account the sustainability of a lifestyle). You guessed it, life caught up with me, reality put me back on another path and, slowly but surely, I regained all the weight I had lost and got back up to 300 pounds.

Why, do you think? With my recent research and the results that I have been able to validate, I understand better and I will explain to you.

In 2005, however, I continued to take the initiatives that had led me to this weight loss of 70 pounds, but I never crossed this plateau of 235 pounds. Never!

Even with this intermittent fasting lifestyle plan, you're going to hit a plateau. It's inevitable and I've experienced it myself. A glance at my weight charts will attest to this. I have often written that we must not make the mistake of repeating the same routine day after day, like a photocopier that prints constantly; and the importance of this statement is vital to breaking a plateau. I have to tell you that I was a little perplexed, but I found ways to improve my situation. The following suggestions are among them.

First, replace the bad oils with olive or avocado oil. You could also abandon industrial carbohydrates in favor of natural sugars, and eliminate toxic consumption such as carbonated soft drinks.

However, the real solution that satisfied me lies in two options, associated with your new lifestyle regimen of intermittent fasting:

1) Stop fasting and start eating more normally three times a day again. It is suggested to do it for around ten days, but I did not have the patience to wait two weeks; so I did it only two or three days, before fasting again; and it worked really well.

2) Extend your fast longer than you have done so far, and in another area; It will break your current routine.

The idea is to cheat a little with your own body, which is used to undergoing what you have imposed on it for a while. So, I ate in larger quantities for two days, before moving towards a minimum fast of 36 hours. The plateaus are gone and here I am slender, at 185 pounds in June 2024. You could also add exercises of your choice, especially after 15 hours of fasting, where it pays off. Your body needs a reset to start better.

MY CHOICE: The plateau presents itself and I choose of my own will to eat normally for two or three days, even if it means fasting for a minimum of 36 hours afterwards.

YOUR REFLECTION: Prepare yourself mentally, be ready to be resilient, because this plateau will blow up in your face sooner or later. However, there is a simple way out and you have to believe in it to break your routine and thus outsmart your body.

Good and bad foods

If you are thinking of adopting this new lifestyle regime focused on intermittent fasting, do not expect a miracle pill like those pills that abound in charlatans' advertisements and other methods motivated by greed. If you don't want to change anything in your eating habits, the results will not be convincing. If you don't change anything, be sure that nothing will change. After a while, your body will get used to it as it always does naturally. You will be surprised to no longer want to eat bad foods, by choice and because these "bad foods" will make you feel downright bad.

I was surprised to find that I didn't feel well following my first real breakfast after a month of intermittent fasting. I wanted to treat myself to a lumberjack breakfast with the traditional bacon and eggs, but it was not as rewarding as anticipated.

Oddly, afterwards I hated how I felt. Mentally, I felt like I was stopping to lose weight. I repeat, the way you break a fast is as important as the fast itself. One doesn't go without the other, and with this line of thinking you need to make a list of vegetables you like, proteins to favor, and good fats to balance it all. Don't be surprised to read in favor of fat, because despite its bad reputation, it is essential.

Salt and fat are the unfavorites of traditional diets that don't work, when in fact both are absolutely necessary to meet the needs of the human body. If you watch the television series where participants are sent to the Arctic Circle to try to survive with a few tools and a tent, after three or four weeks of hunting rabbits in the wild, they all find themselves lacking in fat.

The body needs fats, quite simply, but good fat. Even if the participants who killed and ate a big animal, they need fat and they go looking for it, following in the footsteps of the classic caveman. I come back again to our ancestor who had no medical knowledge to validate anything, and who made do with what he found on his path.

We are this caveman still today, and really not the denatured one who stuffs himself with sugar and junk of the modern era all day long.

What humans put in the animal's stomach when it grows, we consume, and all this beautiful chemistry comes from our stomach's ability to kill bacteria. I can't claim to have done this literally, but I've cut my meat consumption in half and, what's more, I save a ton of money when I get to the supermarket checkout. You should keep in mind that fasting will lower potassium, magnesium and calcium. Salt is not an enemy.

If you start doing research, you're going to get your money's worth by learning who wants to sell you what. On the other hand, by relying on my credible sources, I managed to incorporate a few new products and eliminate many others, without suffering. Strangely, I discovered the benefits of certain bitter-tasting products such as ginger, sauerkraut and radicchio. When I eat tuna, I have radicchio leaves instead of bread and I love the result, not to mention my liver thanks me every time.

Studies have shown that ginger is rich in vitamin C and magnesium, which are stars in a fasting state. Daily consumption of ginger will reduce inflammation in your intestine, have beneficial effects on your skin and speed up your metabolism. Nature offers you these products. It's up to you to decide what you need to change in your diet, because one thing is certain: you need to change it. If you add two grams of ginger to your meal, it is proven that you will burn more calories digesting that same meal. In addition, ginger helps generate less fat and reduces your hunger cravings.

Never forget that the gut is your second brain. It is necessary to have the useful bacterias because the intestine metabolically releases all the nutrients into your blood system.

Fasting gives your intestines some well-deserved rest, just as it once did for the caveman waiting for his next kill. Your body contains 15,000 to 100,000 billion cells and as many bacterias. Think about this for two seconds: we are a megalopolis of bacterias. There is a symbiotic relationship between bacteria and humans.

Most prescribed drugs flow through the bacteria in the intestine, where they are filtered. Those with cognitive impairments such as occasional brain fog often have intestinal inflammation, caused by poor nutrition. Welcome to the diseases of modern man, accompanied by a series of pharmaceutical prescriptions.

Fix your gastrointestinal system and suddenly your brain will start working better; it is scientifically proven and validated by myself at 61 years old. These inflammations cross the barriers of the brain. So instead of taking tons of pills, change your diet and start fasting gradually to find your comfort zone. You will heal naturally, be more lit, have more clarity, lose weight and have energy to spare. Stop eating every two hours. Your distant ancestors did not do this. Do not eat in the evening, like your ancestors who could not for safety reasons. Return to the roots of it all, to the base, because we come from the caves despite our modern comfort.

You should definitely avoid foods that contain sugar and cause your sugar levels to skyrocket. Otherwise, it will be more difficult to get back into the profitable zone of fasting that burns your fat. For my part, the domino effect happened when I ate poorly, often and a lot. I had difficulty knowing when to stop.

***Today, I dread these bad foods not only for my weight, but for their fat-burning harm*.**

Let's get one thing clear: our body changes fuel from sugar to fat much more quickly if we ate well the day before than if we wolfed down a pizza accompanied by poutine.

Without further ado, here are the main points of my choices.

The right foods

Before moving on to my list of foods, I would like to remind you that hydration remains the key to success in any diet. But be careful! Water, just water, sometimes adding electrolytes.

- Vegetables, roots or not. I got to know a few of them during my research.

- Sweet potato. It is actually not sweeter than the white potato. However, this potato generates progesterone, an ideal intake for postmenopausal women.

- Locally raised and grass-fed meat, turkey being number one.

- MCT oil, made from coconut oil or palm kernel oil, is easily incorporated into your coffee. It seems that black coffee gives you more energy when you drink one or two cups. MCT oil also helps stop any food cravings that may arise.

- Fish such as fatty salmon for omega 3 fatty acid.

- Organic berries such as raspberries, strawberries and blueberries.

- Avocados, plums, beans, chickpeas, tomatoes and cucumbers.

- Sauerkraut, lemon, lime, ginger and radicchio.

- Despite its many qualities, honey should be consumed in moderation. A teaspoon from time to time will provide you with a little magnesium, phosphorus, zinc, calcium and iron.

- Cabbage, broccoli and fermented foods: kefir, yogurt (without sugar), kimchi.

- Walnuts and almonds.

Bad foods

Eating well means condemning junk food, but if I have a weakness for a juicy double hamburger even today, although it is a food to be avoided, I eat it, however without fries or soft drinks.

Here is a short list:

- Anything that contains sugar: bread, pastries, cereals.
- Flour.
- Anything that contains manufactured vegetable oil.
- Fries, chips and donuts. In fact, anything that goes in the fryer.
- Processed meats and cold cuts of all kinds.
- All juices sold in stores, with the exception of fresh juices made on site with real fruits.
- Margarine and trans fats.
- Cereals and dairy products.
- All carbonated or energy drinks, without exception.

It is important to read the ingredient list on a product carefully, as they are placed in descending order of quantity. Additionally, avoid corn syrup, which is high in fructose, as it directly attacks the liver.

Strong desire to eat carbohydrates?

To begin with, it is up to you to accustom your body to getting rid of this guilty pleasure. The first step is to stabilize your sugar level and avoid eating harmful foods such as those listed just above. They possess exactly everything that is toxic, including bad oils, and they make you want to eat them again and again, as if your belly were a bottomless pit.

Eating sugary cereals or a donut in the morning gives you that instant sugar rush and makes you want to eat again around 10 a.m.

Gradually decrease your food consumption hours to naturally increase your fasting hours. Make sure your last meal of the day contains enough protein and fat to avoid sugar cravings the next morning. I often had breakfast with toast or a bowl of cereal. I now start with a large glass of water, then a black coffee with a little MCT oil, and I'm gone for a while, without any side effects.

This is the basis of my intermittent fasting: all my mornings go like this. Nothing could be more false than the old saying that the most important meal of the day is breakfast. It is the most important one for the food industry, obviously, but not for our health.

Reducing stress is crucial and essential, regardless of your lifestyle and diet. Find a time and place to decompress. A walk in nature, a cold shower, meditation, reading and soothing music are just a few ways to lower your level of anxiety in the face of the changes you are imposing on your body. I chose yoga and meditation to fill this need.

Monitor your sleep: another essential element for your system to achieve a certain balance. Of course, the longer you fast in this intermittent fasting lifestyle, the more hunger cravings naturally disappear. The body gets used to everything, even the healthy choices. I would even say that you will change your habits completely, easily and naturally. Ultimately, your digestion will benefit greatly and you will gain energy.

Pressure from friends, family and loved ones

When you're working to lose excess weight, those around you seem to encourage you. But is that really how you feel? You may have 100 pounds to lose, lose just 20 and you'll be warned: "be careful, don't go too fast," "a little at a time," etc. Weird, right? But in fact, that's not the truth, we probably just want to please you.

All our lives we are programmed to associate pleasure and happiness with food and drink. When you receive an invitation to dinner for a mega feast with friends, the meal lasts all evening long and the wine flows freely. That's quite a dinner! We enhance this concept in everyone's thinking. Then, when our turn comes to host, we want to do more and that's how we have fun. We take pleasure in slowly making ourselves sick like the modern man of today.

I won't dwell on children's nutrition. They are growing and they need to eat properly and with limitation. Our mothers were for the most part excellent cooks, and as a Quebecois, I must admit that we ate in large quantities and quite regularly. Among all my childhood friends, abundant food seemed to be a common denominator.

We get invited to a friend's house, an uncle or a brother: what do we do? They offer you something to eat and drink, a beer, a bowl of chips and we treat ourselves. What happiness!

We organize a party that we want it to be memorable for the guests: it is preferable that everyone leaves satisfied and stomachs full. Holiday season, public holidays, vacations, weekends: so many perfect excuses and excellent opportunities to celebrate like a king, a modern man version let us point out.

There is also the Pavlov reflex, a theory relating to the conditioning of humans to carry out activities or to have certain reflexes acquired through learning. These habits become reflexes when the brain makes connections between the stimulus and the resulting action. All the media and our wonderful governments are in cahoots with multinationals to push us towards excessive consumption with a huge pressure group ready to indoctrinate us. The more of us there are, the more we consume. We thus become the victims of these multinationals who sell us just about anything.

As a worker, you are entitled to a healthy break in the morning and another in the afternoon. Which means snacks: one at 10 a.m. and the other around 3 p.m. All this on top of your daily healthy meals, including the so-called most important meal of the day, breakfast. But what rubbish! You watch some football game or the Super Bowl: you eat chicken wings and chips. You go to a baseball game: you eat a hot dog. And so on. It doesn't stop. Everything is an excuse for food consumption.

What I have just written, I have experienced throughout my adult life. This led me to watch my weight go up and down on a roller coaster, often climbing up to 300 pounds. Now at 185 pounds, do you honestly believe that I could suggest that you associate pleasure and happiness with excessive eating? No! Impossible for me; This is no longer my case. With all the wisdom of my 61 years, I can discern the nuances of life with hindsight from my past choices.

We cannot go back in time, but we can control the present and plan for a better future.

I don't regret anything about my past life, but I never want to return to those weight levels that prevented me from doing the activities I always loved and, therefore, from being happy. Today, I do whatever I want. No dinner invitation is too tempting, no event can stop me. I chose to follow my lifestyle because I feel better. It's a simple matter of choice.

Something else. I assure you that you will be provoked by someone in your immediate circle. Be prepared to remain vigilant and follow your course of action. Nothing stops you from doing all the activities, from chatting, from dancing, but pay attention to the fasting or eating period that you assigned to yourself at the very beginning of your new lifestyle regimen. Also make sure that this does not harm your happiness in any shape or form.

Why not treat yourself to one of your favorite meals every now and then! This is the beauty of this lifestyle: it is designed by you and for you. Pizza and spaghetti are my two weaknesses, my guilty pleasures, and I admit that I sometimes spoil myself while remaining in control. Strangely, you will see that the more your health and well-being improve, the less you will taste these whims of the past. It's like your body turns a corner and realizes that your stomach doesn't need to be stuffed like it used to.

Three lessons I learned with wisdom:

1- You should not regret the past, because you cannot change it.
2- We should not live in the future, because it is proven that 90 % of what we believe or hope for in the future will not happen.
3- You have to live in the present moment. We are largely responsible for our very own happiness.

MY CHOICE: After several months of my new lifestyle, I made the decision to follow my game plan and only drink water during special events. Quite simply because it makes me happy.

YOUR REFLECTION: When you are confronted by a loved one who is lecturing you, or invited to a party overflowing with all kinds of food and drinks, what are you going to do? Ask yourself what makes you happiest.

Types Of Intermittent Fasting

This book recommends that you create your own lifestyle regimen by following intermittent fasting. The first question to ask yourself will relate to reducing your time window in the day; like: what will be your feeding period? Are you going to skip breakfast and only eat at lunch? What time will you allow yourself to eat lunch?

Lunch becomes the meal that remains stable, unless you only have one meal per day or you go for a 36-hour fast. The idea is to give your stomach some respite, some rest. This is a good way to lower your sugar level in order to get your body to draw on its fat reserves for fuel.

If you want to lose weight, digging into your fat stores is like winning the lottery; I guarantee it.

For my part, there were periods in my life during which I did not eat breakfast often because I was in too much of a hurry. So it was natural for me to start with an early morning schedule. Especially at dinner, as there are often several of us at the table, our presence is obligatory.

Before looking at the most popular types of fasts, you need to learn to walk before you run. Let's go with a classic example: if you eat breakfast around 6 a.m. and eat dinner around 7 p.m., that then gives you a window of roughly 11 hours of fasting, including your night's sleep.

With that in mind, you have to find a way to increase these 11 hours of fasting, by stretching them into the rewarding zone of at least 16 hours, to obtain all the benefits.

This would be the first big step, without a doubt, and it can be done slowly. Why would you be in a hurry, after having probably lived since childhood according to the famous government food guides?

Think about it, could you have lunch at 7 a.m. instead of 6 a.m., and dinner at 6 p.m. instead of 7 p.m.? If so, you've just gained two more hours, and you would reach 13 hours of fasting.

You understand the principle and all this can be done slowly but surely, because there is no rush. By taking this first step, you will perceive a feeling of well-being in your body; maybe you will even lose weight.

You need to compress your eating times during the day. The rest of the time, drink water, black coffee or herbal tea. Are you feeling a little hungry? Grab a big glass of water and tough it out. It will dissipate... A few minutes of patience and you will no longer feel it.

Every day you need to think about when you will start eating and when you will stop. This exercise is in fact the only one to which you should pay special attention. I mentally note this time every day.

No need to repeat the same scenario day after day. As I explained in another section, you need to vary the fasting periods and break the routine. Out of the blue, something unexpected happens on my way: a pizza tickles my senses? I jump on it, telling myself that in the next few days I will do a 24 or 36 hour fast, promising myself to get back to the right foods quickly. And that's it!

I feel in full control as if I had a button to turn my impulse on or off. So this pizza has no effect on my weight and it makes me happy. Life is beautiful!

In the past, my weight problem was caused by the amount and frequency of food I could eat. I paid no attention to everything I ingested throughout the day. I even went so far as to snack in the evening.

From 12 hours to 3 days of fasting

Before listing popular examples of type of fasting, here is an overview of what happens to our body during fasting, depending on the number of hours of dietary restriction chosen.

Between 12 and 16 hours of fasting

During this period, your body will change the way it burns sugars. You will begin to shift from sugar fuel to fat fuel.

At 17 hours of fasting

Autophagy begins its work and a recycling of your old cells takes place naturally, like a free repair. Your body cleans itself, including purging cancer cells if necessary.

At 24 hours of fasting

Your intestines and digestive system regenerate. This will cause your brain to function better. Remember: your gut is your second brain.

At 36 hours of fasting

This duration is ideal for weight loss: your body will draw fat from places that have not received attention for a long time.

At 48 hours of fasting

Studies have proven that the dopamine system is rebooted and the signals sent to your brain to make you happy are received by new receptors. Food eaten after this period will taste better and give you great satisfaction.

At 72 hours of fasting

Your immune system is rebooted; nothing less!

Daily variation of fasts

Some examples of fasts will follow. Note that you need to vary them and not get your body used to a routine. Otherwise, it will reset its metabolism anchors and it will not necessarily give you the anticipated results.

Types of fasts I have used and still use:

- 18 hours of fasting

Probably the most popular, it allows you to eat lunch at noon and dinner at 6 p.m., without breakfast. You will get fast results.

- 16 hours of fasting

It may suit you if your schedule does not allow the previous one.

- 24 hours of fasting

Only one meal per day.

- 36 hours of fasting

The latter may seem impossible to you, but after you get started, it will become easy.

Obviously, we can go up to 48 or even 72 hours. For my part, I have not yet crossed the 72 hour mark, but I intend to do so. For the moment, I am completely satisfied. That said, you should never say never.

Other popular types of fasts:

- Only one full day per week.
- Two or three alternate and targeted days: Tuesday and Thursday or Monday, Wednesday and Friday.
- 72 hours twice a year.

The easiest way is to create your own type of fast. For your health and well-being, you will adapt your new lifestyle and type of fasting to your situation. After all, it's up to you to discover what's behind fasting. Take your health and future happiness into your own hands, because you are the only one responsible for it. So make it a priority.

The simple fact that your new lifestyle was built by you will change your entire attitude. The quality of your lifestyle regimen will stand the test of time and, over the months or even years, you will be in full control of your life.

The muscles

Here I am at 187 pounds after having lost 115. Yes, I melted. It's time to start working my muscles. I must continue practicing the activities listed above.

We always think of judging everything by weight, but my good doctors tell me that our sugar level and the condition of our arteries are even more important than the number on the scale. I certainly agree, but up to a certain point. For the big Johnny that I was, the pleasure of seeing my weight go down was too strong for me to listen to them. Now is the time to think about moving more even if my yoga cuts me perfectly to my liking. My body has strengthened so much: I feel like I am 20 years old.

The more muscular you are, the more insulin-sensitive efficient receptors you will have and you will thus strengthen your mitochondria. As we age, we become more refractory to insulin. It therefore happens that people aged 40 and over begin to gain weight without changing anything in their diet. Life moves on...

Another thing: if you are having difficulty making the change to the keto diet (the ketogenic diet), for example, increase your weight in the gym and add muscle. Please note that I will never become an accomplished bodybuilder. I really like having a body that allows me to do all kinds of different activities. That said, make sure you don't get too thin and keep an eye on your muscle mass on your journey to a better world.

Obviously, you have to do daily exercises and I invite you to do the one you like. This will contribute to your enthusiasm for your new lifestyle. Humans are made to sprint and get out of their cave: to run after their prey and then hide. Besides, 40 km marathons and multi-hour endurance races aren't exactly in our DNA.

After thinking about it, I noticed that marathon runners often looked like they were going to die at the end of their race. In contrast, sprinters like Usain Bolt, like tennis players, hockey players, football players and athletes in other disciplines, put in short but intense efforts before resting.

Which ones do you think look the healthiest? We must therefore prioritize more intense physical activities for 30 or 60 minutes, followed by well-deserved breaks. In the way of our ancestors, in short.

The Kenyan Eliud Kipchoge, marathon record holder, and the Jamaican Usain Bolt, the fastest man in the world over 100 and 200 m.

A little tour of the planet

South Asians have a 7% risk of developing heart problems in their country of origin, compared to 2% when they are on American soil. So, a three times higher risk in South Asia; and same thing in India. On the other hand, Americans rank first in the world for all coronary heart disease and diabetes.

My good doctors also confirm to me that there are more diabetics among us than we believe, because the method used here to declare a person diabetic, underestimates the reality.

It takes a decade in prediabetes to officially become diabetic. It often starts in your early thirties. Diabetes and sugar represent real pandemics. We are not supposed to eat every two hours, nor are we supposed to eat food manufactured by machines and marked with barcodes.

Why am I taking a little trip around the world? Because of ethnic differences in diseases; there can therefore be no universal treatment. A Chinese person who has high blood pressure will likely suffer a myocardial infarction or heart attack. A Caucasian man with the same data will have no problem. A black man will have kidney problems. They're all different ethnic genetics with the same disorder, though. We are all made differently. The shape of man is today modified by hormones which have never seen so many harmful foods in our intestines. Sugar is undoubtedly the world's greatest poison.

Also, on the planet there are places where people live longer than the world average. These places are called "blue zones". Some examples: Sardinia in Italy, Okinawa in Japan, the Nicoya Peninsula in Costa Rica and the city-state of Singapore. Most citizens of these places enjoy a life expectancy that exceeds 100 years. What we need to understand is the relationship they have had with food all their lives.

Go watch the relevant documentary about it on the web and you will see a Costa Rican citizen over 100 years old who remains active, working and looks only 70 years old. To summarize, during their lives these people only consumed natural foods, whole grains, vegetables, beans, sweet potatoes, legumes and nuts. If you eat a cup of beans a day, you'll live four years longer, at least according to this documentary. Nothing less!

To exercise, these people do not have a gym. They are physically active by doing their household chores and growing their own food.

We have our healthcare system with our food guide that can make us sick, while they have absolutely no need for it. We believe ourselves to be civilized, modern and intelligent... So let's learn the secret of their longevity! People in these blue zones also cultivate healthy lifestyle habits like having fun, dancing, laughing, drinking wine, and living happily with friends and family.

Do you remember the four steps of my new lifestyle regimen? One of them advised reconnecting with friends and family, because the road to health also lies in our hearts, and our happiness in general in our environment. We waste billions of dollars on gyms, nutritional supplements, medical prescriptions, but we must put value in the simple pleasures of life. Don't wait for your governments to keep you healthy and to make you live to be 100 years old, you yourself must create your own blue zone, which is in fact the main theme of this book.

It's still quite crazy to see that living simply, even in poverty, is preferable for our health to the modern life we lead in North America. Unfortunately, the latter values money too much, which allows us to eat, drink and consume to satiation. But ultimately it makes us sick and kills us. Live simply and you will live longer and happier. What a wonderful concept!

Measure your glucose level

I admit, I never check my glucose level, but I should. My good doctors tell me that we should all have a continuous glucose monitor to monitor our glucose as needed. There are inexpensive models of blood glucose sensors that can be applied to the arm near the shoulder and connected to your cell phone for a complete analysis. In fact, the possibilities are quite numerous, but we must reconnect these sensors occasionally.

This way you could know what kind of food affects you. Since everyone is different, one food can cause your sugar level to spike more than it does with your neighbor, despite eating the same amount of the same product.

Same thing for a diabetic. He or she must constantly test himself or herself using a small device, the glucometer or blood glucose reader. It also has the option of a single-use lancing device. As for me, I don't like needles. I prefer to be tested twice a year in full by my family doctor.

By the way, my last health check was perfect, serving as validation. Even though my family doctor thinks that my new lifestyle comes from the planet Mars, he told me: "Nice job, keep going, everything is normal and perfect."

Honestly, I rely a lot on my own feelings and sensations. My weight loss has done so much good for me that I really think I'm on the right track. However, I didn't think I could lose 100 pounds in such an amazing and easy way. But measuring the glucose level is a good idea. I strongly suggest you do it, because it will really give you an immediate indication, with a number to validate your sugar level.

Another interpretation of fasting

In the history of humanity, fasting has been practiced by almost all civilizations. The Egyptians, Romans, Greeks and many other nations used it to detoxify the body and improve the clarity of the mind.

Fasting can completely transform your life, and depending on the direction you take your lifestyle, you will feel younger and younger.

Additionally, some religions use fasting to some degree to illuminate the religious experiences of their followers. Although I am not very religious, I admit that fasting has a long history and its benefits are not new. But in modern man, industrial agriculture puts a wide variety of products within our immediate reach; many of these products create at least a moral dependence. It's up to us to think about what we put on our plate to sustain ourselves.

Regardless of whether it was done for religious or other reasons, there were benefits to reducing calorie intake.

The animal kingdom is also filled with species expert in fasting, such as reptiles, penguins, bears and even seals; they can continue to live for months without food. Bears even drop their heart rates by 80 % during hibernation. But in our modern world, the practice of fasting has demonstrated that we can increase our life expectancy and, thus, push health milestones back into the more distant future. In other words, take full advantage of a longer, healthy life.

Before the agricultural revolution, around 10,000 BC, food was not as available as many assume. Humans have involuntarily become accustomed to fasting, a reflex essential to their survival. In today's age, several studies demonstrate the benefits of intermittent fasting on obese people, those who are overweight or even those at normal weight.

A multitude of studies carried out over many years on animals have shown that calorie reduction and calorie consumption intervals have a direct effect on longevity; not to mention a reduction in the incidence of chronic diseases.

Even the American Diabetes Association, around 2017, stated that fasting could trigger cell recycling; this recycling is called "autophagy".

Autophagy, a word of Greek origin which means "eating oneself", occurs after approximately 16 hours of fasting. The body turns against itself when there is no more food coming in. In autophagy, the body literally takes the bad cells lying around and transforms them into energy for fuel. As if nature had planned that human beings would often lack food for indefinite periods.

I am able to experience the sensation that accompanies autophagy, when I am in fasting mode for more or less 24 hours. It is so beneficial that today I choose to fast to carry out certain tasks or activities, because I feel better than if I had eaten. It's that strong. Autophagy is like removing waste from your body. And with fasting, there is even more waste that turns into energy.

We can improve our health, mental clarity, weight loss, hormonal fitness, and resting gut. A period of fasting causes regeneration of our cells, general detoxification, while emptying bad fat from our body. What more could you ask for and, what's more, for free?

Recent studies show that fasting reduces the risk of a range of diseases associated with old age; it even becomes a prevention.

You will live longer and healthier, with a better quality of life; I personally validate this for you. When your insulin level is high, you become refractory to insulin; just like a diabetic. But to live a long and healthy life, we must be sensitive to insulin so that we need less insulin to regulate the amount of glucose in our blood.

If you associate fasting with a bad state of mind in which you fear fainting and falling ill, I assure you that the opposite will happen to you. But this book is not aimed at type 2 diabetics! If you do not suffer from diabetes, you must fight this moment when you will be hungry, take a glass of water with a pinch of salt and, depending on your current state or what you have eaten before, you will fuel yourself so that your fat turns into amino acids, which will form proteins used by cells throughout your body.

Please consult the section which clearly describes the benefits of each of these fasts depending on the number of hours chosen. Obviously, when fasting exceeds 48 hours, growth hormones and stem cells are generated in greater numbers. And all of this is given to you for free by your body.

Consult your doctor if in doubt. Even if few doctors will agree with you, it's always good to start a conversation. I did it with my doctor, at first fearful but then happy to see my new results.

The gut microbiome

Of all the human organs, the most neglected, although the most important, is undoubtedly the gastrointestinal tract. The digestive tract has connected neurons, controls everything because of the signals they emit, and some experts affectionately call it: "our second brain".

It is also proven that 90% of the signals sent from the intestine go directly to the brain.

All fasting experts – including my good doctors – talk passionately about the gut. Everyone agrees on its importance and everyone seems amazed by its functioning, its complexity and its great contribution to our general well-being. Many naturopaths preach fasting of even up to seven days to perform a total reset of our intestine. In general, the longer the fast, the more your body recharges and the more your gut's natural healing mechanisms kick in.

Before embarking on a long-term fast, please consult your doctor. At the risk of repeating myself, it is always important to fast for as long as possible. However, it is also important to know how to break this fast in order to optimize your health.

For all those who, like me, have eaten poorly for years or have often taken antibiotics, or for women who take the contraceptive pill, the effects on the intestinal system are firmly anchored, frozen. You need to repair your system like restarting a computer. The protocol is to start by fasting for 24 hours to allow the bad microbes to disperse.

The good microbes that enhance growth hormones and regulate your glucose levels will then begin to grow and flourish, as you create more space for good cells. This fast of just 24 hours can even cause you a little constipation or mild diarrhea, because the bad microbes no longer have their usual environment. Ideally, we suggest breaking the fast with bone broth, but I do it with my favorite vegetables or with pieces of chicken or tuna.

You have the choice between taking concrete actions now to improve your intestines, or condemning yourself to suffering from many of the diseases that affect modern man.

Obviously, we all want to live to be at least 98 years old, being able to walk down the street on a beautiful sunny day. So, the choice is yours!

Obesity hides several afflictions. You have to know how to attack it not only to have a better life expectancy, but also to enjoy a better quality of life at all times. There is evidence that those who eat every two hours have a much more damaged microbiome than intermittent fasters.

We should eat fiber and fresh local foods, as well as fermented foods such as sauerkraut and kimchi. For yogurt, try kefir as well as omega-3 supplements, as they will also help your bowel functions. We must ban or reduce vegetable oils containing omega-6 and everything manufactured in industrial factories. Omega-6 polyunsaturated fatty acids can be pro-inflammatory, but they also have beneficial properties. You be the judge.

Our body contains 10 trillion cells and 100 trillion bacterias. So, we are made up of more bacterias than human cells. The countless bacterias in the gut produce chemicals, and what comes out of them is fascinating. Each of us has a microbiome and our intestinal system will simply be the barometer of our lifespan on this planet.

An apple turnover with that?

As dessert for this book, I cordially invite you to refuse all apple turnovers and anything that contains sugar. You will understand that it was a joke. Just have a glass of water for dessert, please. You have seen the harmful effects of sugar on your health and, sincerely, I think that our governments should make sugar illegal if they really cared about our health. But they are more interested in turning the economic wheel than protecting our health. Sugar and vegetable oils are the big stars in my book, the kind of stars you want to run away from.

Your future and your health are in your hands. Take full control of yourself, without relying on anyone; especially not on food guides. Be wary of information conveyed in the media that promotes unlimited consumption. Create your lifestyle plan: imagine it, see it, dream about it, write it down and, above all, start it. It's a cliché to say that you have to take it gradually and one step at a time. This rule applies perfectly to intermittent fasting... The first two days will be the most difficult.

Go for it! It's worth it!

Afterwards, you will slowly become more comfortable, everything will become normal and you will be able to stretch your fasts easily; and all this for your very own well-being.

You will be surprised to feel your body talking to you, rejuvenating, giving you new energy and renewing itself, naturally and for free. Your brain will be livelier, brighter, clearer, younger, even renewed, and you will quickly feel the direct link between this organ and your intestines.

The final word

The preface by Sylvain Guimond, Ph. D. and high-level expert, dealt with several psychological aspects of human existence. Here, I leave you with two epilogues written by two men very close to me.

The first is my favorite Latin and French teacher, Laurent Delainey, who was a real source of inspiration for me: he pushed me to write and to love words. In addition, he was responsible for junior golf at the Sorel-Tracy Golf Club during my youth. He was a good friend of my late father, Léo-Gilles.

The second comes from my best friend, Yves Parenteau, with whom I grew up in Sorel. We played hockey, and we made all the bad moves in Sorel at the time together.

Yves knows everything about me, including my weight problems and my sporting successes. He even witnessed my intermittent fasting in person, as I took a five-day trip in the midst of my weight loss with him in October 2023.

If you remember my four steps, a trip with my best friend Yves was one of them. Yves – Toto for short – has been diabetic for a long time and we discussed at length my discoveries on controlled intermittent fasting, thanks to which my good doctors have been able to help many diabetics.

MY CHOICE: Continue this lifestyle until my death, because I am now in full control of my life and my self-esteem.

YOUR REFLECTION: Has this book tickled you enough for you to try some form of intermittent fasting for a few weeks, just to see what it can do?

I invite you to consult my website: www.jeunejohnnyjeune.com

The latter will see the light of day slowly, not quickly, at the pleasant pace of my life, a pace that I have set for myself and that I invite you to follow. This site will one day offer products, services and even conferences.

Hopefully, you will hear our theme song when you access the website. I don't really have a goal other than to have a little fun, write, create and share my knowledge and lived experience.

I have already won and obtained what is most important to me in life: HEALTH.

With that, thank you for reading me. I wish you a good fast and I raise my glass of water to your health.

Namaste!

Epilogues

Laurent Delainey

Laurent Delainey was born on January 24, 1943 in Saint-Robert, a suburb of Sorel.

He studied for 15 years to become a teacher: in elementary school from 1948 to 1954, in secondary school and college from 1954 to 1960 and at university from 1960 to 1963.

At the age of 20, he became a teacher at the Sacré-Cœur school. He taught catechism, English, biology, geography, decorum, Latin and French.

In 1981, he moved to the Bernard-Gariépy high school and retired in 1998. He therefore spent 50 years in the school environment.

From 1975 to 2012, as a hobby, he wrote for the newspaper La Voix and now, since 2012, he has written a column for Sorel-Tracy Magazine (STM).

"Mala malus mala mala dat." The bad apple tree produces bad apples.

Laurent was a good apple tree.

As head of juniors at the Sorel-Tracy Golf Club in the 1970s, I knew Johnny Larochelle, the brilliant young golfer who set records that have still not been equaled to this day.

Then, I had the chance to count him among my Latin students. This is because he was brilliant enough in French to be admitted to my two groups interested in perfecting their knowledge of this mother language. Years passed and Johnny became the founding owner of Superpunch, a thriving embroidery machine and embroidery supply service business. If everything worked well on the business level, on the personal level Johnny experienced serious problems with being overweight at a certain point in his life. A few months ago, he made the decision to lose weight. He started reading and finding out about all the diets generally offered. He chose intermittent fasting. Accustomed to succeeding in everything he does, he regained his healthy weight in a few months. So happy, proud, he decided to share his experience with the readers of a book on intermittent fasting.

In short, the life of Léo-Gilles and Réjeanne's son is a series of success stories. As his father would say if he were still alive, they haven't seen everything!

Laurent Delainey

Yves Parenteau

Sorel born, journalist and retired trade unionist, Yves Parenteau has been my best friend for over 50 years.

-11 after 13... and the sky fell on his head!

Golf fans will have understood that 11 shots under par after 13 holes guarantee an exceptional round. Why talk about this sporting feat in a book on nutrition, fitness and healthy lifestyle habits? Because we have all once experienced the ecstasy of a good start to a difficult, large-scale project. In life, at work and in sport, it is not the one who quickly takes the lead who must be monitored, but rather the one who slowly and surely progresses lap after lap or hole after hole.

I played this round of golf with Johnny when he was at the peak of his sport in the NCAA ranks. Johnny, a childhood friend since elementary school, my most loyal friend for 55 years. He was so well prepared for this exceptional round. More than 10 years of training, clinics, lessons, readings, high-caliber competitions which have made him progress to this level of performance. There are no natural talents that will make you win anything without all the hours spent learning, training, putting yourself to the test, daring to take the means to succeed. Without effort and without daring, natural talent is an empty promise.

Golf is not only the trigger for his new lifestyle, his motivation to get back in shape, it is also from this sport that he draws his most precious tools: learning, putting it into practice and dare, against all odds, to continue until the objective is achieved. Johnny approaches questions of lifestyle, nutrition, and fitness as if he were showing up one fine April morning at the Augusta National Golf Club, Bobby Jones' masterpiece, to take part in his first Masters. He will be ready, determined to take part in the four rounds of the tournament; he will do anything to win it and the only thing that could stop him… would be if the sky fell on his head!

At -11 after 13 holes, Johnny was heading for a round of 59 of a par 72. But a huge storm leaving a foot of water everywhere made the course unplayable. This score will never be counted because the round was not completed. Too bad because it's an extraordinary feat. Like the one he made in overtime at the Junior Masters in the 1980s, finding himself a few feet from the hole while his opponent sent his ball directly into the hole from a bunker near the green to win the tournament. Lessons that he will remember for all the other challenges of his life. With his efforts, his preparation and his audacity, only the sky falling on his head can prevent him from continuing his path towards the objective.

A week of road trip in the American Midwest in the fall of 2023 with Johnny allowed me to see that he was taking the means to meet this personal challenge of losing 100 pounds, of literally changing the way of eating and to get in shape. Despite certain fasts of 18, 24 and 36 hours, he never lost his good humor, nor his physical and mental strength during this journey. He can watch you eat without being the least bit annoyed. This method fits him like a glove, without causing any unwanted side effects for those around him. It inspires me. Will it help me lose weight? I don't know anything about it. What I know is that the preparation, audacity and perseverance of my childhood friend Johnny, and perhaps his method, are winning conditions to get there... if the sky doesn't fall on my head.

Yves Parenteau

Bibliographical References

Here I have collected the links that allowed me to learn about intermittent fasting and its effects on health.

Dr Pradip Jamnadas
https://m.youtube.com/@pradipjamnadasmd

Dr. Mindy Pelz
https://m.youtube.com/drmindypelz

Eric Simard
Doctor in biology and researcher.
www.vitoli.ca

Printed in the USA
CPSIA information can be obtained
at www.ICGtesting.com
LVHW012312151024
793759LV00010B/130

9 782982 276000